GETTING HIGHER

GETTING HIGHER

The Complete Mountain Poems

ANDREW GREIG

Introduction by RODERICK WATSON
Illustrated by JAMES HUTCHESON

EDINBURGH

For all my friends in the mountains –
thank you for the days.

•

First published in Great Britain in 2011 by
Polygon, an imprint of Birlinn Ltd
West Newington House, 10 Newington Road
Edinburgh EH9 1QS

www.polygonbooks.co.uk

ISBN 978 1 84967 192 1
ebook ISBN 978 0 85790 025 8

British Library Cataloguing-in-Publication Data
A catalogue record for this book is available on request from the British Library.

The publishers acknowledge investment from Creative Scotland towards
the publication of this book.

Design and illustrations © James Hutcheson
Printed and bound by Gutenberg Press Ltd, Malta

Facsimile material from the National Library of Scotland archives - many thanks.

Recordings of 'Interlude On Mustagh Tower', 'Entering Askole',
'The Loch of the Green Corrie', and sections from 'WESTERN SWING'
can be listened to via: www.poetryarchive.org

FIRST THERE IS A MOUNTAIN
Then there is no mountain
THEN THERE
IS

The True Scale of Things
An Introduction by Roderick Watson

> *This is the truth of it:*
> *bunched together on crumbling handholds*
> *under a crazy overhang, the wind*
> *screaming personal demons,*
> *the snow outrageous, night setting in.*

(from 'Captain Zen', *Men on Ice*, p. 21)

Journeys through extremity, both physical and spiritual, are among our oldest metaphors for finding and reconnecting with ourselves in a material world that is both immeasurably ancient and alien to us, and yet so essential to all that we are, or can be. Andrew Greig's *Men on Ice* opens with three Himalayan climbers, 'Grimpeur', 'Poet' and 'Axe-man', facing the void while haunted by the possibility of a spectral 'fourth' in their company, a hipster Buddhist 'Zen climber', also known as 'The Bear'. This fourth presence (Greig tells us) echoes the line 'Who is the third who walks always beside you?' used by T. S. Eliot to signal his sense of a spiritual immanence still somehow surviving in the waste land of modernity. (Eliot had read about a similar hallucination in Ernest Shackleton's account of the hardship he and his men experienced in Antarctica.) With such perspectives in mind, Andrew Greig's symbolic characters will engage in the hallucinatory, free-wheeling, irreverent exchange that is *Men on Ice*: a metaphysical debate about the living moment, dense with allusions, echoes and, indeed, 'fragments' from philosophy, mythology, literature, pop culture and rock music.

I remember how exciting and how remarkable it was to see a book-length poem-sequence of such ambition from a young Scottish poet in 1977: a restlessly brilliant, elliptical, romantic, mythopoeic (and cheeky) homage to *The Waste Land*, from a writer who was equally at ease with contemporary American poetry, most notably Ed Dorn's *Gunslinger* from 1975.

Fifty-five years after Eliot's opus, *Men on Ice* was tipping its hat to early modernism while also channelling the Black Mountain poets, MacDiarmid, demotic Scots and contemporary counter-culture. Nor should we forget that this was five years before *Lanark* appeared in book form, and only nine years after Edwin Morgan's *Second Life* was published: important realignments were starting to happen in Scotland.

Undoubtedly modernist though it is in form, the Romantic (in the literary-critical sense of that term) grounding of Greig's vision is equally clear:

> *What form of life is it*
> *that uphauls itself*
> *out of its element*
> *to icy heights where the sun burns*
> *and lungs heave*
> *to thoughts unnatural and places inhospitable*
> *to countless lives lost by accident or design?*

(from 'To Get Higher', *Men on Ice*, p. 63)

But then again, as if to counter any claims to the sublime, *Men on Ice* is irreverently energised by its ceaselessly changing linguistic registers, in a crowded carnival of references, jokes, bad puns and typographical scatterings to create a phantasmagorical literary space of rock, ice, dope, dreams, caves, raves and the Dionysian drive 'to get higher'. It is unmistakeably a young man's poem, occasionally a little too self-consciously hip, but it was also a strikingly new and welcome voice in Scottish poetry. In fact, with the benefit of hindsight, we can see its style anticipating the verbal energy and the referential excess of W. N. Herbert in the 1980s, or the pop-cultural prose energy of Des Dillon in the 1990s, or Alan Bissett's novels at the end of the century.

Greig's fascination with climbing as a metaphor persuaded the Scottish mountaineer Mal Duff that *Men on Ice* had been written by an experienced rock climber rather than a keen hill walker. On being disabused, Duff took the poet ice climbing in Glencoe for a true baptism of fire: by 1984, Greig was on an expedition with Duff and others to tackle the Mustagh Tower in the Karakorum Mountains of Pakistan. Greig's account of his experience was published as *Summit Fever* (1985), which has since become a deserved classic of mountaineering literature. Further trips to Nepal followed in the company of his then partner Kathleen Jamie, whose accounts of her own later travels in those remote mountain communities were published as *The Golden Peak* (1992), later reissued as *Among Muslims* in 2002, and *The Autonomous Region* (1993). Such is the power of the muse to set small stones rolling on a steep slope.

Greig's prose writing frequently features his love of remote landscapes, not least the bones of his native Scotland, and in his brilliant debut novel, *Electric Brae: A Modern Romance* (1992), this is interlaced with an exploration of what it is to be a man in the company of other men in a sometimes demanding environment, countered by a need for mutuality, friendship and indeed tenderness, as his engineer protagonist recollects a passionate love affair with a complex and creative woman. In this and subsequent novels, Greig's conscious intent has been to provide a counter-argument to the masculine brutalism and the largely urban settings of so much modern Scottish prose fiction.

The more straightforwardly autobiographical mountain poems in this volume speak with eloquence about Greig's continuing engagement with climbing and friendship. Nor should we underestimate how difficult it is to capture the nature of physical effort as well as these verses do. They do not seek the symbolic scope of *Men on Ice*, but there is a striking metaphorical power to many of Greig's lines: – 'in these high places we are melting out / of all that made us rigid' (from 'Interlude on Mustagh Tower', p. 79) – and new and disturbing perspectives – 'and we believe / the true scale of things / is the entire mountain / hung mirrored in our shades' (from 'Back Again', p. 78). Later poems such as 'Tom Ban Mor' and 'Knoydart Revisited' have even more to say about memory and experience, that 'inner mountain' in the landscape of our personal lives: 'it seems you too live twice, / once as participant, again as witness' (p. 207); and 'there are some hills and people / we cannot return to, / because nothing would be the same, / because we never left them' (p. 201).

When *Western Swing* appeared in 1994, it marked a return

to the metaphysical landscape of *Men on Ice*, but this time the long poem was directly modulated by Greig's actual experience of Himalayan expeditions, 'with our tents, our trash, / our high ambition' (from 'Back Again', p. 78). Subtitled 'Adventures with the Heretical Buddha', *Western Swing* takes us once more to the wild places of Pakistan and Nepal, not to mention the 'Up Down Disco', a favourite haunt of Himalayan climbers, which is 'the most sweaty, sleazy and sordid night club in Kathmandu' (p. 193). The book's title signals an even stronger commitment to music and pop culture, but also a more mature reflection on how the West meets the East and on the tensions between tourism, terrorism, consumerism and subsistence living. The section 'In the Last Village' from Part III, for example, is reminiscent of George Campbell Hay's unfinished poem *Mochtàr is Dùghall* (*Mochtar and Dougall*), in which a Gael and an Arab discover bonds through their cultures' common experience of religious discipline and cultural dispossession:

> 'No,' we said gently, 'we do not want
> to come and see you "make the folklore",
> no, nor take pictures of your daughters
> miming prettily in the fields.
> These travesties are painful and must cease.'
> […]
> 'My country too has empty glens,
> old walls crumbling by the sea.'

>> 'We did not call it " folklore" then.
>> We called it nothing but our way.'

(from *Western Swing*, p. 149)

Among acknowledgements made in the preliminary pages of the first edition of *Western Swing*, Greig thanks Philip Hobsbaum, who had asked him, 'What is the true voice of an educated East Coast Scot of your generation?' After some thought, Greig's answer had been 'Many voices.' Many voices indeed, for the protagonists of *Men on Ice* have now morphed into Ken, Stella (formerly the Poet – the character has now become female) and

Brock. The 'Zen climber' has become a 'secret sharer', a 'Heretical Buddha', and the poet has produced an even richer polyphonic bonfire of voices, registers, allusions and references. He calls the process 'sampling', by which a wealth of echoes and traces are layered in the text just as the recording industry cuts and pastes clips from other musical sources into new digital mixes.

No doubt Eliot and Pound would be surprised to be hailed (at least according to Greig) as the inventors of digital sequencing, but in fact the analogy with modernist allusion holds. The author's endnotes list dozens of borrowings, but they by no means exhaust this echo chamber of plural voices. The effect is exhilarating, bewildering, hilarious, opaque, scintillating and moving by turns. Passages in *Western Swing* are reminiscent of the eclectic exuberance of Edwin Morgan (I loved the idea of a 'MacDiarmidtron'), and for all Greig's postmodern awareness, the rumbustuous verbal energy of his verses can also claim an ancestral connection to the inexhaustible Bacchanalia of Sydney Goodsir Smith's 1948 masterpiece *Under the Eildon Tree*.

Nor is it all a playful whirl, for underneath the gleeful pace, there are coded signals of a more profound personal anxiety. After all, the prologue begins:

> I am afraid
> There is much to be afraid of
>
> Bad enough on good days
> when jolly fishermen strip legs from living crabs
> and you wince how that must feel
> and glimpse how quick we're guddled
> from first cry to last gurgle
>
> Worse: waking alone
> in a large bed in a small country
> with a pain in your chest
> and the sea going on and on
> like the auld haiver you'll be
>
> if you're spared

(from *Western Swing*, p. 94)

There's a new sense of mortality in these lines, as well as a political awareness, and a clearer sense of a theme that was always there (if between the lines) in *Men on Ice*, now recognised as a kind of heretical Buddhism:

> *gather round, bairns,*
> *for in this hand I'm holding*
> *a traditional Truth:*
>> *The futility of Desire.*
> *In the other – the heretical*
>> *Truth of its beauty*

(from *Western Swing*, p. 128)

In an interview with the present writer in 1992, Greig reflected on his understanding of the Buddhist position – 'Life is suffering. Suffering has a cause. The cause is desire' – and wondered whether desire is the great mistake in life, or the very stuff of life itself. It is true that Buddhist monks seek to escape the snares of attachment, but neither the artist, the poet, nor the mountain climber can live without the material world, nor forego its beauty, nor the flame of their longing for its ambiguous nature.

> *'In this country, at this time,'*
> *Ken said, 'if you haven't anger,*
> *you've got nothing.*
>> *And if*
> *all you've got is anger*
> *you really have got nothing.'*

(from *Western Swing*, p. 176)

And yet it is at the height of passion, at the height of risk, 'bunched together on crumbling handholds / under a crazy overhang', that we glimpse the ghost of transcendence, that secret sharer by our side, and conceive the drive to write about it.

> *'What language quickens our page?*
> *Desire & Fear – that dual blade*
> *striking upward to the heart.*

(from *Western Swing*, p. 122)

The symbolic blade that excises desire, that cuts our ties to the real (the very blade that's missing from Ken's sheath throughout the tale) reappears at the end of *Western Swing* in the humble form of a tartan penknife, 'A PRESENT FROM AYR', handed to the protagonist in a last encounter with the Heretical Buddha at a fish-and-chip shop in Pittenweem. After such a vertiginous imaginative trip we have finally come down to earth only to find that this, too, is good.

The return to Scotland in Part V is a return to the everyday; the quest in exotic foreign lands – the up and down disco, indeed – is over, and the company has dispersed. Yet this is still a reconnection with the spirit, even (or perhaps especially) to be found in the mundane corners of the East Neuk of Fife. The journey out (which is also an inward journey) has been followed by a return, perhaps (in Eliot's words) to know the place for the first time. These are the 'debatable lands' of the Border, but also the debatable place of Scotland itself and what Scotland will come to mean to those of us who live here.

This concern is a recurring theme in all Greig's writing. It can be seen in the later mountain poems, for example, and especially clearly in the meditation on landscape, art, personal history, geological time and friendship that is the true subject of *At the Loch of the Green Corrie*. Towards the end of this memoir of Norman MacCaig, he writes, '. . . it is time to reconnect to the real thing. Which, whatever they say, does exist. Even if it evades you whenever you open your mouth.' And here, too, the key is to explore the relationship between being and landscape. Or rather the puzzle of being in landscape and yet somehow *not* in it, which is where we all find ourselves, as thinking beings cast into the world.

> *Matter,* he sighed, *is condemned*
> *to eternal push-ups and goodbyes.*
> *Everything*
> *   is nothing mostly*
> *even your physicists know that.*

(from *Western Swing*, p. 187)

Or, as another section in *Western Swing* has it, 'There is a cure for loneliness / it's in the voices that keep company / your place after midnight' (from 'Meanwhile: A Cure of Loneliness', p. 117). In context, this is a comment on the value of friendship, but it might also be the best last word on the many voices of *Men on Ice* and *Western Swing*, and on the imaginative, geographical and spiritual spaces that have been covered in a trip that is irreverent and profound by turns – out and back again with a vengeance.

Roderick Watson

Hold m tight, babe

In the early seventies, after midnight Edinburgh fell silent: all pubs and clubs closed; no TV, no texts, no emails, no phone calls, no internet. My single bed was narrow, and I might as well have been in a sleeping bag in the mountains as I lay reading, writing, remembering and getting higher. *The Twilight Game* (sole surviving draft abandoned) marks the moment when mountain imagery first broke in.

I had published two collections of 'sensible poems', naturalistic, controlled, short. They could not reflect much of what excited me then: '*The Waste Land*', Ed Dorn's underground '*Slinger*', Captain Beefheart's gobbledygook, the onrush of rock and roll, drugs and sexual experience, my attempts to grasp F.H. Bradley and Wittgenstein, and Dougal Haston's exploits on rock and ice.

While still at school, I had written a play of sorts, *Inexplicable Events Near Carstairs Wood*. It had grown from phrases lifted from a Higher French reader ('No, your tie is too gaudy', 'When I was young, we had two pear trees. Both have since been cut down') crossed with Fife back-country ploys shared with school friends. It was silly, improvised, crammed with bad puns, references, accidentally and purposefully inaccurate quotations and spelling, garbled memories.

One night I re-read *Carstairs Wood* and found myself re-imagining it as a mountaineering quest. What came out was not sensible. I wasn't at all sure if it was poetry. I only knew it was fun and felt right.

I showed some of it to an illustrator and musician friend, Jim Hutcheson. He passed twenty pages of text and half a dozen drawings to Charles Wild at Canongate. To our astonishment, Charles said, 'When can you have it finished by?' It had not crossed our mind that a proper publisher would look at this stuff.

The time, care and money – that full-colour cover! – spent on this odd and commercially implausible book come from a different age. Something of that time still resides in it, in the white spaces, in the snow between the rocks.

AG

These men on ice!

MEN ON ICE

Being the story of 3 Climbers
and ... *another*

DEDICATED TO DOUGAL HASTON, CLIMBER

THE TWILIGHT GAME Pt.1.

The voices tire and I retire
to my room and close the door;
turn off the light and then the night
rears up like a wall.

Uneasy movements in the small bed,
I claw my way up, hour by cramping hour,
till round dawn I bivouac at the Camp of Sleep
and roped in rest fitfully in the early hours.

O but it's wearisome climbing nights alone,
you can't take turns at being leader.
I am always up front, I am always
tail-end charlie.

I went to the love-shop to buy some pitons
but she hammered them
into my head & asked why I was in pain.
They're for climbing the wall, stupid!

PROLOGUE
on finding *Men on Ice*

NO CAMERAS!
    Axe Man was adamant.

Don't need no Real-to-Reel Recorder
to tell me I've been there,
I ken that fine.
     (There's some who every step
     must take a picture
     to prove to . . . who –
     themselves?
     they took it.)
We've heard enough
inanities from the Moon,
Aw Mi Gosh Whit A View!
—that's just a post-card
saying 'Wish You Were Here'
when you're not.

I've got nothing to say
to anyone who
wants to know what
I've got to say
when I'm up there.

Yon 'South West Face' boys,
only two interested me –
Haston wi' the pale blue eyes
who doesnae gie a damn
       for pictures
and auld MacInnes,
hauled off wi' snaw in his lungs,
'the fox of Glencoe'.

Ah but the Public
's got a right to know
      murmured Grimpeur
      condescending low
—if they can find us.
That's why
I've left my sketches and
Poet's notebook
waiting in the snow.
Let's see what they make of it.

'Wonderment and fear must be the prime ingredients.
So the pilgrimage becomes an adventure.'

'In the mountains the shortest route is from peak
to peak, but for that you must have long legs.'
—Nietzsche

'Thereafter sleep claimed its way and I moved
gently into another World of tangled dreams,
eased by a gentle flow of oxygen . . .'
—Dougal Haston, Everest S.W. Face, Camp 6

INTRO

Let us define the terms of the game.
There are 3 on the ice-face,
Grimpeur, Axe Man, Poet.

They share the apprehension
of a fourth
estranged yet familiar
like the image in the mirror,
building the same world
the other way round
stretching out his left hand
to greet us
from the other side of the ice—

the *Zen Climber*
erstwhile 'The Bear'.

     Into the shifting spaces they inhabit
     let us drop a little time
     and join them
     in the Ice Fall

     A moment of crisis
     at high altitude
     20,000 feet
     and in the thin air
       their voices
           carry . . .

CAPTAIN ZEN?

'But what is this to camel drivers smoking hashish?'

This is the truth of it:
bunched together on crumbling handholds
under a crazy overhang, the wind
screaming personal demons,
the snow outrageous, night setting in.
Worn down by a maze of dead endings,
baffling reversals, hopeful pitches
turned awry, the future terrifies,
it rears up beyond the vertical;
nor dare we look down
where the past glistens below
— a wicked diamond beauty –

Now each according to his nature
Marvels at his fate –

     Ma axe is USELESS against this
     wall of BLACK ICE! gasps Axe Man.

   CORRECT Grimpeur observes,
   Is this the END?

  Can it BE wonders Poet,
  Not even a WHYMPER?
     and he struggles with the urge
     that surges through the vein
     straight to his brain
     to lean back, let go,
     fall out with a final shout—
     luckily he can't stand pain.

I am G., let me
give my reading of this situation.
We three, touring through time
after our individual hearts' desire
seeking: splendour in action
     the final image of evening sun

       the golden thought,
     are finally come to grief. It seems to be
a terminal case of entropy . . .
       Poet
lost his typewriter
to Goat-Foot's satyrs—
no more Sky Writing.
       Axe
abandoned his monkey-wrench in the Factory
a victim of the Metal Disease—
no more plumbing the Ocean Depths
     I, Grimpeur
my thoughts are pale and dry
as the wind-bleached grasses of Winter
no more sinking in lush pastures . . .

      —Don't give me that golden stuff,
                    Axe grunted
            hammering in
                his last piton,
    Ah've had a great life.
    On the ball
    in the bed
    wading in wi' ma axe.
    Life is a gorgeous tit:
    I wanted to feel it,
    I felt it—
    Phauggh! It was pulsating.
    Now I've sucked it dry
    and I'm ready to die.

  I see   Poet sighing
as frostbite crept along
his finger bones,
    my poems have been all wrong.
    Instead of climbing the wall
    they decorated it.
    I never used one word
    when two would do.

Shall I never sit down hereafter
  to exercise this gift
  and render this disaster
    into Poesie so subliminal swift
    Mood arrives ahead of its master Meaning,
    as lightning does sullen thundering?

No one answered
and silence fell
between those loquacious pilgrims.

        Well, a man's gotta do
        what a man's gotta do
            as Herr Hitler said
            breathed Axe
            with sardonic leer.
        Pax, brothers. And he signed goodbye
        to life's parade
        as he prepared to leap—

        —But LOOK! The Zen Climber!
        Can he SAVE us?

            ah boys   you seem
            to be tied up here   chuckle
                Grimpeur pass me your HEMP ROPE
But Zen
  our situation is IMPOSSIBLE

            precisely   that's the first credible thing
            you've said all day   murmured The Bear
                cutting up Hemp Rope & stuffing it
                in pipe with hairy thumb   in this case
            the appropriate action is

                        Inaction
                        or
                        Action 'In'
            For you suffer from reality vertigo
            the view makes your head spin

does it not
here have a SMOKE
and with a little aid you'll spot
that crack on your left—
it opens into Plato's Cave
there we may shelter
in some safety undisturbed
save for the passing
of the odd philosopher . . .

Mmm.
    Ahh.
    Comfy!
        Pass round the gentle persuader.

    This cave has remnants yet
        of myth & magick, observed our Poet –
    my eyes are drawn
        to glowing sketches on the walls
        I see here the myth of Er
            and is that not Mithras
                at which Axe stares?
Huh,
messy, grumbled Grimpeur
it's cleaner in the
        'Philosophical Investigations' . . .
                That may be so remarked Zen
                but Wittgenstein was a head of his time
                and his time is ahead of ours
                    he passed this way often
                        '*alive with fiery breath*'
    Pass the funny pipe
        mumbled Axe, never much one
        for this sort of conversation,
    Last time I felt like this
            it was VE Day
    and we'd drunk a bottle of pain-stripper
            in toast to peace eternal . . .

what—smashed again
  murmured Zen
    crawling to his sleeping bag
very well
      let Poet tell a tale
  and then goodnight
          my dizzy heroes

POET

POET'S TALE

    Axe Man's hollow stare
    was drawn straight to that portrait
    of Bull and Bull-slayer
    on the wall of our Cave-dwelling . . .
    many a strange likeness flickered there
    as I told an old tale in a new telling . . .

So, at the appointed time
this bloke shows up with a woman
        who is young, beautiful
        and in love with him
    and he is clean cut, respectful to his elders
    and very cool
The labyrinth he figures it out
with a little help from
what was her name
goes right in there
sword in one hand
in the other a rope
    He keeps going forward
      eyes blue & frozen
        till the heart of the matter
          comes out at him
            it was hot it was angry
            it was the real thing
            it was no man's brother
            it was the great ding-a-ling
        till Theseus pushed his cool sword
        into that furious heart
        icicle into a fire &
        the beast is at peace

            the labyrinth is real quiet
            just a little water
            dripping
              the Hero can almost
              hear himself
              think
              (?)

But he doesn't.

And so returns:
        Senators wish to meet the exterminating angel
        the Public touch his clothes
        and buy their children
        little swords and minotaur masks.
His steady ready lady
at the other end of the rope
has done her bit
  and he splits
      then her island is real quiet
      till warm Dionysos moves in
        looking like an Australian
         (bronzed
           boozed &
             bollocking)
      —but she's just the lady of the tale.

They said it was
going to his head
and it was
        but not like that
  No, under that close-cropped hair
  was a banging and thumping and a black despair
  a din and a violence when people came round
  a madness that grew as he walked through the town
                looking round
                  at all the people
                 looking so
                   ugly & down
             he grew hot
             he smoked gunpowder
             his skin got itchy
             he was a midnight prowler

            and when he could disguise it
            no longer
            he left them

      & prowled with his prow
      with the emblem of bull
      a maze of seas
    roaring
    roaring
    roaring

    like a MINOTAUR.

So Poet told his tale
as the last pipe went round. That night
we slept on air.

GRIMPEUR

CAVE MAN

Stripped of Poet's sensual,
animate
and innately religious
wallpaper,
    the head interior
is a cool place to reside.
On the glass chair
  in the very centre of this room
  with 4 white walls
  folded in at the corners
  on which he scribbles with blue pencil
  science's telephone numbers
  for long-distance connections with the Real,
with folded hands
sits the mortician.

  Lest solipsism lead to fear
here is the corpse of a comforting thought;
let us dissect it
with some Witt:
    'We are not alone
     though we are all one.
    For all our dis-parity
    (hypochondriac ghost of my social conscience)
    we are a Community of language-users
    for we play the same games
    and read the tribal newspaper over breakfast.
    What does this mean?
    This means we agree
    on the assignation of names
    to feelings that remain private
    on the basis of public display.
    This means?
    This means I can know
    what you feel
    but I can never know
    how you feel it

only you and God
          (whom others might honour
          for long life and leisure
          to sink in cool thoughts
          in this calm cave
          my Cambridge college
          so far below the mountain tops)
     know that.'
I cannot tell you stories.
My analysis is offered as cure
for insomania.

          Some hours later.

O Sleep
why hast thou forsaken me
when even the Axe Man slumbers?
I could touch him awake, my brother,
across space he'd sympathise—
but no nearer; the deepest crevasse
is that which lies
between one head and another.
Alone, I turn to fight the brain at midnight.

          Existentially speaking
          Grimpeur remains a 'Cave' man
                    remarked Zen.
          Does he not know that's a cul-de-sac?
          Outside the wind still rages,
          the light hawk is tethered to the air.

AXE MAN'S CONFESSION

I got this
     hot
in ma head
when people came round
they tangled together
like forests
whispering
   shutting out the good light,
   the good sound.

Once I walked intae
the Town Library
in search of lightening
but it was I who bolted
from reading-room gloom
where shelves sag under weight of
dead wood.

     Ma mates swayed home
     arms round each other's shoulders:
     thick-
          ets
     they rubbed guitars in long squeaks.

The family circle closed round me:
Grow roots, or we'll choke ye.

     In time I tangled wi' the Copse
     for I,
               I was the good woodcutter
               with my bright axe
               I thinned the neighbourhood
               felled the old and rotten
               carved up the creepers
               pruned the young girls in their bloom—

AXE MAN

It's good to see land cleared.
Quiet. I like that. I'm a
country boy at heart,
I told the jury
in ma best English.
When I grow up
I want to be a hunter.
I like to track the savage animals.
They look at me
with knowing eyes.

AXE MAN IS INNOCENT!
Is he fuck.

GRIMPEUR & THE YOBS

You want to know
why I don't like Axe Man, Poet?

When I was young
we had two pear trees.
Both have since been cut down.
But at that time
yobs came from the town
under the fence like wolves.
We were meant to report them,
but they all looked the same
   hair over their eyes
   smelling of crap food
   and sour hunger
   their eyes cunning
   their words tricks
   they killed frogs
      with an air pistol.

One of them said I could
have a shot if I let him
at the pears
so I did
then he pointed the gun
at my head
and said
      Right, ah'm gonna gie you a shott

I screamed I ran
they were forever aliens.

   Now
   look at Axe's eyes . . .

THE BEAR ON POETRY (I)

*Poems themselves are not moving; it's
that a man should write them.*

—Or, of course, a woman,—

—better still!—

GRIMPEUR'S FIRST CELESTIAL ADVENTURE

Friday afternoon. Down school corridors wondering
just when in childhood the golden
key out of the time-zone
had been mislaid
& now sought so feverishly . . .

    'Temperature rising & the
    juke-box blowing a fuse'
    pressed flat in this
    in many suddenly noticed ways
    too little town
    losing half my friends out of school
    and down on the turntable
    spinning when their number's jacked
    then rejected and neatly stacked
    outside the ministry of employ
    along the bars
    sinking jars
    talk talking of women & records & cars
    till their grooves wear thin . . .

    mad 17
    flute of bone
    carrying a rocket
    around in my pocket
    swearing in demonic french
    incense smeared mallarmé
    as my operating manual
    and mal armé I was until that afternoon
    until I took the capsule . . .

      SACRÉBLEU

    Sacred blue! No key
but choirs & choirs
ripping sheets of space harmonies
across the slipstream of the blood

now pounding on the ears
as on an inner door
        —No door!
        Deep in inner/outer space
        free from the gravity of time
        though always circling round it
        the escape-hatch opens
dreamlike slow
the hero spread
eagled in the firmament
where either his head or space is bent
looking up and yawning
up into the awning
wanna i wanna
stay up here
where the day
never turns
into night
How long have i felt this sway

        Hey slam that door SHUT
        & come down at once boy!
        Are you out of your box?

(that must be Janus Janitor
 swimming silver-suited astronaut
 into my field of vision)

Take me to the HEAD
i said
Taken by the ear to the cool
        blue blue school pool
Janus crackling through the tight
helmet of his skull
        Allow me to illustrate
        a parable
        Our being alive may be equated
        with our falling into water

(throwing me in with a
low trajectory)
and our philosophy may be equated
with what we do in there
viz Strike Out In All Directions
Life is not a game
Games are something you may *choose* to play.

Pulled out (blue blue
shimmering on my blazer)
i am disarmed of my water pistol.
Take this stinking rag to the HEAD
muttered Janus to the Secretary as she
took down my particulars with a pencil
i took up my particulars with the merest blush
and dripping was shown into the study
(Quiet you angel voices).

Behind the desk sat the HEAD
His face was a study
i studied it
        Hm—eyes like wheels
            teeth like a trap
            the computer in heat

What's this,
Revelation?
Not in my school!   he snarled
Your tie is too gaudy
quit this childish
phosphoressence
you little twat.

        i took off my tie
        it was certainly a hallicimat
        (total dissociation within 2 seconds).
        There are no ties   i noted
        that is your collar troubling you
        no viewer need be troubled
        for there is no EYE

NO I! gasped the HEAD
Why that's terrible!

i turned to depart—
No one may leave here without permission!
Very well well said i
call me creature of the stars
call me this nothing
you call me this astro nought
in your eyes i am no one
and this i may leave without your
scabby permission

What of Original Sinn
screamed the HEAD fortissimo
    and shivvered azure beading on my cuff.
    Very well
    i wish to consult the blessed krishna
The Blessed WHO?   crackled the HEAD bursting
                into platinum flame
                glowing like the burning bush
  Wrong!
  The Blessed WHY
  There is no
  doctored who

Thus it came to pass
the HEAD blazed in the desert
of his parchment
& i left school for good
                good
                    good

i was not consumed

                there is
                no
                consumption

And thus, concluded Grimpeur
kneeling at the last embers of our fire,
Did I first get higher
and take my first step on the trail
that somewhere in the mountains ends
and tonight finds me campèd here with you,
my Friends.

That day we climbed no axe, out of our skins.
Axe wedged his points in gnarly times,
cranked his axe
torqued to th max

gave it baldy, got physical.

And when he reached his limit and was spent,
Grimps cleared his throat, asked
'Why they are rente whom you
can brush a stroke of talent
up the cliff?'

Then he went & de-contorted it
and when the mountain re-assembled we
was so much farther up.

ON FALLING

No, Poet,
people are feared to fall *off*
and *out*
   off the ledge
   off the boil
   out of sight
   out of their minds
You be sure and fall *in*
and you'll take deep rest
in your deep-ression
when you fall as we all do
right down some terrible night
the spirit of gravity
locked round your shoulders
down through all the levels
into the ragged hole
in the heart
of the heart

then
when you can fall no further
when everything is permitted
but nothing is worth it
   walls fall away
   mountains are as glass
   wind plays violins
   on the other side of the ice

The eye recoils from nothing
All things shine from within
You never know fear again

You call such men insane?
Their eyes are calm
surviving smoothly in a monstrous environment.

GRIMPEUR'S EXPLANATION

When I gathered from my backsliding
from my one-step-forward-two-back
progress through life
    that life was made of ice
    that life was perpendicular
    that the years became vertiginous
my will became ruthless
I went into my armoury
and started a design for
        crampons

Suitably shod
a man may climb the wall
even walk the ceiling
as Christ did except they called it water
There have been suggestions
that crampons, codeine & cocaine
are unethical aids
that our climb and our failure
must be done alone

O
but my powers
were made to be extended
& O
the high ice
is beautiful beyond belief

Inside an icicle I once saw
green grass preserved
and now the memory floods me

    I am in there
    on the other side of the ice

    I am a zen cow
    I munch miracles all day long

PRAISING THE WOMAN
(Poet)

1
In the morning, blue-white
snow brightness;
at night car headlights,
on the ceiling, flicker.
We lie all day in bed, words
thickening with soft insistence
into the white afghan of sleep.
And when I wake in the darkness
we seem to be purring
towards an unknown, yet certain,
destination.

2
I sit up late by the fire,
wrist-wrestling with thoughts
that remained wordless
for you sleep now and I can
push this pen no further.
Still it snows, swirling
straight from the mountains
to come softing round her house,
a knock or a summons;
in the salt dark the shed door
swings and bangs in the wind.
I put away my books
and soon sleep washes out
the clouded mind, the milk bottle
swirled clean for tomorrow.
In the morning she will rake the peats,
they crumple to ashes with a faint sweet smell.

3
The only thing I know
about love: accept
no substitute.

THE OLDEST GAME

Ah, the assent of women, sighed Poet,
Why don't you blunt your edge there, Axe Man?
So Axe explained as night
slid over the ice.

Ma break came when I wis playing around
wi' the lads   we'd heard there was someone
looking fer talent   I made a few smairt moves
I've aye had style tae ma brut

so she signed me up
Put It There she said
so I did

And in time made her first eleven
an' made ma climb tae fame
putting it in from aa ways
in the heat of the moment nane faster
there wis animal roar
when I wis on the ba'
jist watching the replay
wud knacker ye

There wis some talk
o' long-term contract aye but
ye canna believe aathing ye hear
in this game   lemme jist say
it's magick
when you're big
when you're Up There

Great till wan afternoon I went in
low and hard frae behind
aw I wis provoked but
the wee black book for me

Frae then on I wis nowhere
tried too hard   lost the timing
running a' over the park
niver where the action wis
     time I got there
     it had moved on   I
     couldna get tae the ba'

Na, the ba' game is fer mugs
tae mony folk after the wan thing
Gimme the moonless nights
gimme ma axe

     I play my ain game
     agin the boys in blue
     watch ma style

REFLECTIONS ON THE MIRROR
(Grimpeur)

That is the haunting edge of glass;
the shadow of yourself
peering from the other side.

The light shifts and how
easily the shadow disappears;
the glass is clear
before the pane
the viewer stands alone again.

World within mind
Mind within world
A shift of the light
and the self is uncurled

Out in the mountains
the Mind problem is em-Bodied
in volcanic form:
if every peak is ideally projected
as on some inner silent screen,
what melancholy being is this travelling eye
that ants a way across the icescape?

I quiz Zen,
that mirror image glimpsed in glances,
this mote in the mountain corner of my I;
he flickers back into clear ice,
the prior source from which unfurled
the mystery of self and world.

(If yon's a metaphysical theory of self,
Me Physical Ta very much,
grumbled Axe.
Ah, never mind, Grimpeur,
consoled The Bear,
different foxes for different boxes.

Considering you used words
you stated the thought
in a ploughman's honest clumsy fashion,
holding the horses of the intellect
in a near-straight line
across the crew-cut stubble fields that run
between the golf course and the ocean.)

Aye, very good, Zen.
You'll soon hae Poet
out o' a job—why no
stick to yer rope-trick and the airt
of maintaining motor cycles?

The Bear turned his massive head
and dissolved the Axe Man in his liquid eye.
Very well, he growled. *I like you,*
Stumpy, and your stubborn hand-Pict race.
For a mortal you're exceptional. Now
B. off—I must comfort our Poet.

THE BEAR ON POETRY (2)

So, Poet, your thoughts are quicksilver fish?
And the page the net to pull them in?
Very well: a fine haul
      they gasp and die
      in empty air

You can't eat them all at once
so quick!
      before they rot
      whip the guts out
      with a fishwife motion
      smoke them
      salt them in a barrel
      screw down the lid
      they make a tidy snack
      on winter nights when friends come round
      to do their heads in
      with home-brew

  & fisher of words
  expect shrinkage

the plump & shining thought
when preserved
is brown & shrivelled
and quite quite

boneless

      The true fisherman leaves
      his nets on board
      and lowers himself into the sea . . .

HOOF
THE MUSICAL AXE

Come, Axe, The Bear requested
as the last light rested
over the gloom of the Western Cwm,
Mak us Musik on yon silvery 'axe';
sweet music to unwind the mind
and hone the clouded judgement,
for today lies weary in the bone
and tomorrow is as yet unknown.

And so that physical man
with the head of the Hashshashin
complied, reached forth the hands of power
to play away the slack-tide hour
of aimless sorrow, that drifts
between the ebbing of today
and the rising of tomorrow;
his thread of melody sewed a seamless suture
between the present and our future.

Yet the healer as so often
was not healed
but all the while revealed himself
in the false fire of a memory flash
of a different land
where first his senses reeled
under the overtowering Rock Band ...

... T.A.M. drop out from the rain badweather
violent hair en brosse stomps through The Door
to the music of a few 100 guitars and SLAM turn
those lights down   sweat crawling
from his toe-nails   but they can't! In the confused vegetable-air
scent and sweat slide across the leather skin of ...
The Lizard holding down bassguitar forked tongue slitting
between his lips as he
leans back

on 500 Watt Stax
with his elongated 'axe'
booming up like concorde
(mania is his reward)
and surveys with satisfaction
the action
below . . .
Young Tam's eyes bulge as white strobes lobotomize
his lobes Turn Those Lights Off! slashing time & motion
into classic frieze of assassins & assassinated and my
god there's bull's horns on that HOOF that lead guitarist's
head & he roars as
                        200 weight of Middle C
shoot up the iron girders on the fat roof & the
Band Slam
into thundering boogie WILD THING . . .
rhythm-bass-drum 50 ton o' loco-motive, running on
violent lines just WHAM WHAM and again WHAM remorseless
inarticulate protest slamming heads back against walls
imprisoned in 4/4 time till
we can stand this confinement no longer and HOOF
now
      Stepping Out
                        forward and Up
into a cage of white light a dog shameless
leather guitar swinging erect the lean
silhouette lifts endlessly as HOOF
emerges from his lair in white heat lets   'fly'
screaming volleys of starshell notes
into the night of that sadistic SLAM.
Power cords detonate down the spine:
concrete walls of prisoned sound now poised against
                        the 'flight'
of this free agent extemporizing ex-tempo atonal
stone free from time and key hurtling through
clustery meteors showering Down
his white hands blur
like the saw wheel whir
and *he*

claws into *Metal*
Shreeking
and the crowd roar in ECSTASY!

      It is an emotion
that wears boots as Dionysos
lifts the roof in rapture
and the caretaker runs for the polis
& HOOF now pinned forever in young Axe's retina
learns the secret of Electric Guitar viz—
Infinite Sustain and now lets the long
long notes hang
           quiver
                topple
                      hang
        in the raging ecstatic
cry of white birds & soaring
out of the dream factory
one man's mind
swims in an ocean of bliss . . .

      Smoke
rising from the amps
      Sweat
dripping down the walls
truck loads of sound split wide open—The Lizard's
just playing Any Old Thing—spilling over
          shambles of messed fury
                multi-coloured jackals
            pulling apart a wild guitar
              Screaming Mr Every pulls no weight
but searing to the back wall
scratches in hellish delirium for reason
      HOOF is building smokestacks through the smog
        as *flames* lick up the Stax
        and his axe
          EXPLODES
      & *freezes* him there on the Summit
          crackling with electricity

                & shattered head
                    hazed in blue
                        as his brains fuse
                            you can hear him
        RAUGGH!

        & young Theseus screams
        for in the engine room things suddenly
            go wrong &
        120 tons of fuzz
                    sighing a tremendous groan
            burst through the Factory
        & plug the frenzied half-wits in the corner
                where men and women
                    are
                        dis in teg ra ting . . .

        Yon bath o' ecstasy and death
        all my violence drained
        doon the plug hole,
        clockwise.
        All that remained
        was tae tak tae mountains
        secret as a mole,
        fearin' to be human
        hopin' to be whole . . .

            But Axe explained to them no more
            when to his ears came . . .
            unharmonious snore; swept
            in a rare moment of despair,
            he wept while the others slept.

NEXT MORNING
'Morning in the Bhyundar Valley . . .
the mutations of the universe are apparent'

Good morning me!
thought Grimpeur
crawling from his sleeping bag.
Snakelike I slough off the skin
my night-self inhabited.
Ah sing us a song, Poet, a Lay
of the morning arising
over the mountains
of the preceding day.

O!

          (the Poet's cry leaped
          from his lips and ricocheted
          from peak to peak
          and each time echoed back
          more beaten out and bent
          till finally a shapeless sound
          like dew dispersed and, spent,
          sank into the ground . . .
That's all?

    How may I elaborate
    on Zero?

Huh?

    Sweet,
    sweet fuck all! laughed Axe,
    tuning up his 'axe'
    but for the benefit of this
    intellectual, this grimpeur
    who asks What Was That?
    even when he's been there,
    pray elaborate whiles I air
    ma G string

and for our tenancy in this day, pay rent
wi' music to delight the sense
that wi' the heart experiments.
O: a cry of ejaculation
   my cry of joy on this crystalline dawn
   waking in fractured heads
   as yet innocent of thought or desire
   clear as the air up here
O the very picture of the self
      the hoop of fire
      unending stimulus
      enclosing nothing
      yet given shape by it
      as is the rainbow by the air
      it bridges

O the original sweet nothing

O is a portal
   through which thoughts fly
   and disappear
   and no one knows
   where they goes
O!

       Methinks Poet approaches his summit
       quoth The Bear, and left his cave
       glowing and strong
       like morning sun emerging from dark mountains.

GRIMPEUR EN FER
'Il faut reculer pour mieux sauter!' —But how far?

We found Grimpeur in a parlous state.
Too smart for anything but words
he'd thought himself to a standstill
roped securely in
a lectureship
        camped 3 floors up
David Hume's Tower
& there he taught on 'possible worlds'
having no grasp
of this one.
His face was blue
his hands too
he looked ready to vote
Conservative—

      'Why, Gramps, you're half-asleep,
      you're about to Drop Off!'
        'Aye,
        the nerveux climber's lost his nerve'
        sneered Axe.

Then Grimpeur turned and for the first
time I felt the
Heat of the man:
      Look hollow eyes you
      vicious little sod
      what know you of *Nerves*
      who've got none
      who've never stood at the blazing
      crossroads of decision
      nor felt the pale two-fingered
      septic hand of scepticism
      tweak the very carpet from your
      cloven feet   and leave you
      sprinting the firmament!
      Hey Tam

your violent body's brave enough
and I'm afeared of it
but dropped into my *mind*
you'd soon be lost a-mazed
'alone & terrified'
and sobbing beat your
so-called brains out
on the midnight labyrinthian wall—

a season on fire
is more than
a systematic derangement
of the stomach
You
wouldn't last longer
than a snowbull in hell,
you'd be—FLASH-FRIED!
LOOK,
(he threw off his ropes
leaned out over the abyss
and let it
wheel into him)
NO HANDS!

But—no words?
commented Zen
You dare?

And revelation grew in Grimpeur;
he fell on his knees and could
not speak
we carried him out
on the red hooves of sunset
silent
thoughtless
free

TO GET HIGHER
(Grimpeur)

To get higher
how many lights
have burned out in the night
the brain at midnight overloading
glowing minds camped high
in top flats of tenement buildings,
lives rising like rockets
trailing fire
to collapse insane on a street in Turin
arms round the neck of Dionysus.
What form of life is it
that uphauls itself
out of its element
to heights where the sun burns
and lungs heave,
to thoughts unnatural and places inhospitable
to countless lives lost by accident or design?
Climbing into life
or out of it?

Back in the homelands
escapism is the charge,
fear the stimulus,
I the religion.
Escape from concentration camp –
no blame says Zen.
See how they follow the hero's progress
with bated breath even as they sneer
and put their slippers on.
In the blue TV screen light
they yearn for our destruction
so they can put their shame to sleep
and yawning climb the stairs to bed
too little alive to ever be dead.
Outer space was our thrust . . .
the return was made
with a handful of dust.

So a generation came from West to East
to find the highest mountains
to conquer 'inner space' . . .
(if they could find it).

To Get Higher.
Here we found koans
exits without entrances
monks chanting mantras
on a cherry-coloured morn
polite headshakes and immoveable silence.
They say we use . . .
too much force.
How else can ye climb? asked Axe
Whit kind o' heights are yon
where they don't even show us the mountain?
Let's say we found
guides and sherpas there
to hump our excess baggage . . .
servants who treat us as children.

To Get Higher
so many fires quenched in the snow
eyes obliterated in dazzling madness
friends who disappear
without warning without explanation
on a solo attempt
when the weather turns bad.
And even those who have stood there
with 'the ultimate view'
on the height of personal Everest,
they Neverest. Only downhill thereafter
lucky to cash in the past
with a ghost
writer.
In our colour supplements they appear
burnt out space heroes & mountaineers
Haston Aldrin Lennon Leary
'bearded and anxious'

'hiding behind a remote half-smile'.
I turn my wayward gaze
to the ground beneath my boot;
thinking not of peaks, I loot
them at every turning of the way.
In here and now no step is up or down,
on in pain and hope and joy I go
until I love but do not linger on
each footstep in the snow.

POET'S NIGHT SONG & ZEN'S BENEDICTION
'The snow lies deep on glittering Soracte'

Meander meander
the river is tender
the heart too
tenderest when passing through

    Immortals don't care
    they toss laughter like coins into the pool of our sorrow
    while over us light passes
    night passes
    we pass

Time takes all
as we wait for the death-fall
it's the domino effect
each moment topples the next
right up to Double Blank
    night without stars
    without friend
    without end

Death sits in
on every song or tale or smile
holding the last tile . . .

    Big Deal
    said Zen
    life's too short
    for a long face
    in the wrong place
    You know it, Poet
      Here, hang on to This
      (it's all that there is)
    Tonight we sleep on air
    in the northern city
    the view: glaciers by night
      love to you gentle listener

now turn out the light

sleep tight
don't let the years bite

Aye, Pax,
Brithers. Cast honeyed sunsets
o'er the clouded scene, but pray
don't dull my eyes
wi' all your golden lull
—ah!—
—Bye!—

```
Z Z Z Z Z Z Z Z Z Z Z Z Z Z Z Z Z Z Z Z Z Z Z Z Z Z Z Z Z Z
Z                Z
Z                Z
Z                Z
Z                Z
Z Z Z Z ᶻ Z Z Z
```

GRIMPEUR'S GLOSSARY AND INDEX

G string, Axe Man airs his
God
GRIMPEUR—mispron. 'Gram-Purr', from French
('Climber'). Born of a half remarkable question. The
intellect of the group. Good on thin ice and climbing in
chilly, remote areas. Highly-strung, talks to himself. A loner,
owing to difficulty in conceding the existence of others.
Diversions: dialectics and drawing. His voice: *Legato*.
Hashish, camel drivers smoking
Haston, Dougal, Climber & Scot,. Elements of Axe
(physical courage, anger, endurance) and Grimpeur
(philosopher and introvert).(This collection and
dedication predates his death by avalanche).
Head, of his time, gone to his, interior, not in ma,
gun at my, bent, of the hashshashin, shattered
Hitler, obligatory reference to
Hoof—paragon of lead guitarists, brother to
Axe Man. Flight and death of. See Minotaur.
Hume, David, his tower—Enlightenment
pinnacle of Edinburgh University.
Ice, life made of, other side of, clear, the high
Ice Fall—broken glacier leading into Western Cwm.
Italics—usually indicates Zen's speech.
Jackals, multicoloured
Lizard, The—Hoof's Bass Guitarist.
Mallarmé, incense-smeared,
Minotaur, death of, relation of Theseus to
See also Bull, Hoof.
Nietzsche, collapse of, quotes from
O, analysis of,. See also Zero, Sweet Fuck All.
Persuader, the gentle
POET—born in a field, raised in town. Of limited stamina, but
gets there (takes short-cuts). Secretary and sometime cook to
the Party. Scene-setter, teller of bedtime stories. Took part in
early Epic Expeditions, but later concentrated on lightweight
Lyrical assaults. His voice: *Con Brio*—or possibly *Cantabile*.
Poetry, Zen on What's wrong with Poet's, subliminal swift
Revelation, not in my school, grew in Grimpeur
See also Summit, Spacewalk.

Rope, hemp, uses of
Self, metaphysical theories of?
Smythe, F. S., quotes from
Tit, life is a gorgeous
Thoughts, unnatural, golden, pale and dry, calm,
as a cure for insomania, when preserved,
innocent of, fly and disappear.
Wittgenstein, in praise of, 's anti-solipsistic argument
Woman, assent of, praising the, talk talking of
ZEN CLIMBER—alias 'The Bear'. Eminence blanche to
the Expedition. Reported by Shackleton in the Antarctic
(see 'The Waste Land', Part V), and Haston and Scott
below South Summit Everest. It was Poet who first called
him 'Zen Climber' (and that in a moment of stress), so
his ascription is approximate at best.
Zola, Emile, positively no mention of. See also Freud, Marx,
Hesse, Stalin, Guru Maharaj Ji, Hugh MacDiarmid . . .

An Alien Encounter with the Suburban Kind

from

'Breaking the Ice'

But what is this outlandish balding creature
in Arran sweater and gardening trousers
who climbs his way through swithering snow
towards our resting place?
That hump upon his back,
those leaden weights about his feet,
why does he thus handicap himself?

Another weekend existentialist,
groaned Grimpeur,
hide the absinthe.
This is surely un touriste,
a superfluous physical presence who brings
cheap scenery and non-essential commentary
as he munches a pre-packed lunch
in a pre-wrapped picnic spot,
the dyspeptic victim
of democracy.

(An abandoned sequel - too soon!

THE BAT
(Forward to *Surviving Passages*, 1982)

Poet, could you insert your song
into my ear
a wee bit less fizzingly?
You make my brain buzz
like a faulty striplight
in a motorway café.
What use your labour with midnight oil,
    blazing new routes
into the dark,
        climbing 'The Bat'
in stocking soles
        under ghoulish Glencoe moons
as Haston and young Smith did –
if no one gets the way you went?

Your puns exploded
godawful starshells
that left the night more black.

Those outré traverses
without sinking even one
'deadman' of logic as you
chopped a handhold in the white-out,
those chunks that came
    loose in your hand, lobbed away –

you freejazz climber trying to build on
your bum notes so they ain't
bum no more –
what use if none can follow you
without frostbite in their bleeding ears?

  In short
I fear if you persist
in leaping from peak to peak
like the veritable bloody chamoix,

your audience will tan your hide
and use your poetry for
CLEANING THEIR WINDSCREENS!

   There was a young lady from France
      who entered a tram in a trance...
the wordman murmured in delirious wonder,
knocking snow from his boots,
hung in Clachaig's ingle by their straps.
How may I reply? If words were chocolates
You'd eat all the hard centres.
But I loved Liquid Cherry,
God she was fantastic...

If I could explain to you the sheer
necessity –
               but then
I'd be rooted in this spot forever
for there's not time
to talk *and* climb
and explanation plods on prosey feet.

   Believe only
that though I aim *per verse ad astra*,
I aim not to be perverse. For me
no other combination will suffice
to unlock the heart on fire,
the mind on ice.

So welcome,
         welcome to the multi-verse!

Though it is more sombre since my fall.

Guess round this time I abruptly
fell out one life into another — a long way down,
but worth it.

Early gear list for our 1985 Pilkington Everest
("Unclimbed Ridge") Expedition

1 x Thermal Balaclava.
1 x Thermafleece Balaclava.
1 x Maddur wool hat.
Moon boots — not sure yet depends on cost+offers

2 x Karrimat 5 season.

No. Thermarests.

? M.T. Sac?
1 x Mt Equip Everest S/Bag. These
will be slightly larger than ~~the~~ normal
depending on how tall/fat you are
GTex covered for Climbers
not.   -   for BC.
Kurt + Julie have. N.face Superlight plus.
    (I hope you'll be warm enough!).

  x AB expedition sac LW.

  x Berghaus Red Point Wall sac.
    Special large version (super light.)!
    for Climbers + film team only. — MLT?

Stoves will be camping gaz C200.
with high altitude gas. we have had
to pay for this as they now charge
everybody.

Witco shovels. enough are bought but
if you have one bring it.

Glacier glasses/goggles. we are in P.Wks
control here we must wait to see what

'REAL CLIMBING' POEMS
(from 'The Order of the Day')

A true story, then. Years later I met a real Himalayan mountaineer, Malcolm Duff, in a pub in South Queensferry. He said he'd loved *Men On Ice*, was planning an expedition to climb the Mustagh Tower in the Karakoram Himalayas – would I like to come and climb it too, maybe write a book?

He had failed to grasp the essentially metaphorical nature of poetry. I may have understood yearning and fear, the draw of the summit and the abyss, the joy and vulnerability of the body – but I had never climbed more than a few Munros, and was scared of heights (still am).

After an intense, demanding, joyous and at times deeply frightening apprenticeship, I went on the 1984 Mustagh Tower trip. It altered my life. It led to writing prose and so making a living, to experiences life-threatening and life-enhancing, and deep friendships. I went as support climber and chronicler on three Himalayan expeditions, and climbed through five Scottish winters.

When I committed to the writing life, I never expected real adventures, only ones in the head and heart. Mal was my Bear, mentor, jester, dear friend. His death from a heart attack on Everest Base Camp in 1997 remains a lasting loss to many, and this book goes out to him.

Along with the prose chronicles, these years produced some 'real climbing' poems, where the climbing experience leads, and the metaphorical seconds, removing the protection as it follows on up.

AG

BACK AGAIN
On Lhotse Shar

We're back again
with our tents, our trash,
our high ambition. We've come
to be both audience and show.

Mal flicked his lighter,
an avalanche roared –
we have come to assert
everything fits

and we believe
the true scale of things
is the entire mountain
hung mirrored in our shades.

*

All day snow sank in the billy,
was boiled, drunk, peed, replenished
as we passed the mountain through us.
The chat was home and axes, hopes, seracs.

The voices tire, yellow lights
hiss as night comes on
to very few witnesses
but enough.

Unblinking stars and lightning –
the theatre's hushed.
From the heights we propose
to the depths we've left

our shadows gesture and stretch.

INTERLUDE ON MUSTAGH TOWER

In these high places we are melting out
of all that made us rigid; our ice-screws
hang loose on the fixed ropes to the Col.
Monday in the Himalaya, the clouds are down,
our objective is somewhere, but obscure –
let it soar without us for a day!
We lounge in thermals on the glacier,
brewing and shooting the breeze, that improbable
project of conversation among the living.
Laughter rings across the ice. Why not?
None of us will die today – yon's immortality
you can draw on in a cigarette,
harsh and sweet, the way we like it.
Steam rises from the billy, Sandy pours.
It is true high, worked for, that we pass
hand to hand between us with our brews.
Men on ice, going nowhere and laughing
at everything we cannot see but know
is there – among the cloud, on the Col,
a hand of some sort is tightening our screws.

SANDY, TOPPING OUT ON MUSTAGH

So began to lead the last of the Tower
Quite hard   more bold than difficult
tough ice   loose snow   but soon brain
began to play the game   My points investigated
stabbed   good placements to be had
among loose choss   Crucified by altitude
I bridged a steepish rockwall   Good
value that   I remember everything
like ice-slivers in my windsuit's creases   Camp 4
a thousand feet beneath my heels   climbing
into my shadow   the sun
flashed off my axe
                        Jon he was somewhere
giving good rope and no advice   the ideal second
but me   I was gone

        Nice work when you can get it
        the hardest   the best   hours passed
        till I wanted a think and a rest
        so thumped in an ice-screw and hung out awhile –

                Like I cannot spell, speak porter-talk
                but who does not who's lived like me
                with oil roughnecks and a French girl?
                One look in her eyes, I know.
                One straight hit, I find good ice.
                Climbing's not so much, my life's more in
                the way I eat my food, the man I rise above,
                the roads I drive to friends,
                these suit –

        Re-engaged myself and winkled on
        with patient pickers unlocked the crux
        set my axes well and at full stretch
        pulled over the top and saw into China –

Felt ok felt well
à cheval across the summit
K2 in the distance looking good
Suspicion of moisture behind my shades

Made a belay and took in the ropes
as Jon came up. 'So how's it going?'
Oh, wasted, youth ...

From Base Camp to the stream there is a path now
And the grass is yellow at the centre of the path.

7090M – 2 × O₂
3 × CLIMBING ROPES (1 in BRUNTONS)
2 × FIXING ROPE (UTS' is WAY AHEAD)
ALL THE WANDS
3   DEADMAN
4   STAKES
      SHOVEL
ASSORTED PEGS CRABS ETC.
1 SILLY CAM

26th April
29 April
First Burrell:
      1 TENT
      1½ needsfured rope
      Shovel.
      assorted pegs, friends etc.
        Dead Men
        Snow stakes
      2 Climbing rope.
      2 Marker wands
      1 Stove   1 Pan
      2 Gas   1 Radio

ENTERING ASKOLE

On the eighth evening we entered Askole.
How can I tell you? We had seen
no habitation in two months. Brown dogs
twitched in the shade, a chicken screamed;
we smelled dung, daal, smoke, lentils;
many voices, the bronze fields shone.
Lean as schoolmasters, tall wheat rapped
our knuckles as we limped into the square.

Say there are miracles between
where babies twitch and sleep and old folk
sleep and totter. Water-mills spun,
yaks plonked circles round the threshing floor.
Evening prayers, a sleeping miller, tawny goats
stole husks of wheat. Goitres hung
like apples on the children's necks.
The Hadji lightly touched our backs, *Summit good . . .*

We had been above ourselves, hooked to
pure worlds of black & white & blue,
the narrow world of sleeping bags.
In Askole we smoked and talked till dawn
then rose and crossed the river,
paid the porters, jeep did the rest.
We broke down, sang 'It will come hard
to sleep on beds as soft and wide as ours.'

THE WINTER CLIMBING

It is late January and at last the snow.
I lie back dreaming about Glencoe
as fluent, hungry, dressed in red,
you climb up and over me. That passion
claimed the darkest, useless months
for risk and play. You rise
up on me, I rise through you . . .

The shadowed face of Aonach Dubh
where Mal first took me climbing
and as we clanked exhausted, happy,
downwards through the dark, I asked
'What route was that?' 'Call it
what you want – it's new.'

You reach the top and exit out;
from way above, your cry comes down.
The rope pulls tight. What shall we call
this new thing we're about?
These days we live in taking
care and chances. Why name it?
My heart is in my mouth as I shout *Climbing* . . .

CRUX

Delicate, hell-cat, at the crux on Hoy,
last word in day-long converse
with rock above deep blue, climbing
into pale blue, aiming for grace –
A hard way to be normal. The gods of agility
took him this far, 400 feet, soloing
and high on that mug's game.
Now they desert him. His fingers stutter
below the bulge – he's run out of ways
to speak to sandstone. Gripped? Mummified.
This rock is smooth as political tongues.

Hung from a hand-jam,
rock crystals enquire of his skin
How much you want to live, sweet youth?
Some questions draw blood and pride
equally, he answers, smears his right foot,
gets his left edged high. Chalk-bag,
pinch-grip . . . Now he's kiltered out,
all trussed up and nowhere to go.
The world waits with casual interest.
Gooseflesh, a draught blows through
from the next world – *going there soon?*

Adhesion's mostly faith for intricate movers
but he's shivering agnostic now
releasing the hand-jam he
s t r e t c h e s
                   his right boot slips
right hand up
                   fast as a prayer
grabs his Grail o lovely jug
then cranks like a maniac over the bulge.
Thugged it to the top, sat and was blank,
was gone, was everywhere in Orkney longlight . . .

We met him in Stromness, it was etched
in his eyes he'd dipped into more
than his chalk-bag that day.
White as cocaine his fingers
drummed the bar, awaiting tequila.
'Been pushing the envelope, matey?'
His eyes were mica as he considered
our question, glinting and flakey his smile:
'Aye, licked the stamp too.' Revving kite
on a taut string, could plummet or soar –
delicate hell-cat, you'll do.

THREE ABOVE NAMCHE BAZAAR
heading for Lhotse Shar

Sandy, feeling somewhat queasy,
squatted above Namche,
shat a five-foot worm. My life's
like that, he said as we
laughed and took our photographs,
a thread of consistency
through unconsolidated crap.
           – All things pass
as expeditions through the Bazaar,
joking & jiving & ripping each other off.
Got a bad feeling about this trip, boss.

Some days you scoff and scoff
but just get thinner,
Mal grinned. Had a friend,
dead now, he always swallowed
a tape-worm before he came this way –
never got ill. He'd say
just to be here, we must have been promoted.
           – Think that's true?
A monk once stopped me on the trail
below Temboche monastery, said he
saw death in my eyes, now I'm wondering whose.

We rounded the corner and there –
the big Mothers: Nuptse, Lhotse, Everest.
My heart battered
                in my chest
like a man
             beating
on the walls   of the cage
              surrounding him
       and I thought
                huh   Climbing –
this bad bug kills off all the rest.

AFTER EVEREST

Between one expedition and the next
we buried the tiny Buddha's bones
upright, with respect,
at the bottom of the garden.

Then we were driven
back to the mountain.

Between the highway and the ditch
the restless West
verges on its limit ...

No one said we are too old
to die young, too young to retire
as we left Lhasa in dust.

AVALANCHE

He's at it again,
first time in years
a woman's hips hands eyes,
wherever the categorical resides,
have issued the imperative
Screw our lights out.
Hot bulb! (Cooling in the dark.)

He dreams of avalanche
quick & white & casual . . .

Waking in sheets
he regards her where she lies face down.
The terror lies
in the tenderness derived
between the slope and shiftings of her ribs.

In 1991, in an ouzo-inspired fit, by moonlight I climbed the fence round the Castalian Spring in Delphi, sacred to Apollo, god of poetry. I drank deeply then climbed back out. A few months later, I awoke in Essaouira, Morocco, with a sharp pain in my chest. I had written no poetry in two years.

I lay in a night sweat and a voice unheard in a long time said *I am afraid. There is much to be afraid of. Bad enough on good days, when jolly fishermen strip legs from living crabs* ...

I sat up and wrote it down. In pencil. HB. I thought *Heretical Buddha*. The *Men on Ice* company must be reformed, on a new quest for a totem, a healing Blade, to undo the injuries done by and to us in the intervening years. The whole sequel *Western Swing* began to suggest itself. It would contain Scottish winter climbing, travels in the High Atlas while the first Gulf War was on, memories of the infamous Up and Down Disco in Kathmandu, yearnings for distant Fife. Once again it seemed possible to use everything, to go beyond sensible. To embrace even the inner, ageing Axe Man.

Poet has become female, which seems natural. The mountains here are now part-real, part ghostly backdrop. In the music technique of digital 'sampling', I found a practice I could transfer to poetry. It gives lasting satisfaction to have mooted the MacDiarmidtron, and sampled together Lou Reed, Robin Williamson and Henryson's *The Testament of Cresseid*, and to finally return some of what was owed to '*The Waste Land*' and 'Desolation Row'. Not to mention the Samye Ling monastery near Eskdalemuir, and our conversations there about the dual nature of Desire.

AG

دار المـــغـــرب

VILLA MAROC

—⊰(•)⊱—

UP & DOWN DISCO 1

'Come on over to my place,
we'll be having a party'

The bells rocked down like pieces of cold
and then we went on to the party
at the Up & Down Disco — western swing
was playing that night & every night
beneath the reeling stars & we stumbled quite jazzed
with the soft dark in the streets of Kathmandu.
With the H.B. at my side
I felt free to sing the praises of Devine ...

*Yes, we'll catch
that wisdom train,
but why arrive
early at the station?*
— Bud

WESTERN SWING

Adventures with the Heretical Buddha

DRAMATIS PERSONAE

I: Narrator, reader, witness. Also the Company as collective. Also Ananda (see end notes), Drew. An empty vessel.

Ken (formerly *Grimpeur* in *Men On Ice*): as in 'you ken' or the philosopher Anthony Kenny: a knowing man, the doubt-filled intellect. The head.

Stella (formerly *Poet*): The scene-setter, a troubled young woman, the heart.

Brock (formerly *Axe Man*): A surly badger or Pictish stronghold. The body, and its music.

The Heretical Buddha (formerly *The Bear*): Who's he? If the three principal characters were legs of a stool, the *Heretical Buddha* would be the seat. And *I* would be the one who tries to sit on it.

But already the lights are going down . . .

PART I THE QUEST & THE COMPANY

Prologue – Crossing Rannoch – a Short aside – in the
Clachaig Inn – some words of explanation – Stella writes
from Hospital – A cure for loneliness? – the Axe Man wakes
– Stella escaping – Kenny sends a fax – a 'blue butterfly'?

*Darkness. The sound of the sea. As eyes adjust we become aware of a
reading lamp, a solitary reader, a bed, and a few signposts. Such as:*

PROLOGUE

A solitary speaks

I am afraid
There is much to be afraid of

Bad enough on good days
when jolly fishermen strip legs from living crabs
and you wince how that must feel
and glimpse how quick we're guddled
from first cry to last gurgle

Worse: waking alone
in a large bed in a small country
with a pain in your chest
and the sea going on and on
like the auld haiver you'll be

if you're spared

*

I am afraid of many things
I could make a list
but it would go on a bit

Sleep's out of the question
and you might as well admit it
make tea and sit up in bed

with this sapling's worth on your knee
and roll a cigarette because though you're afraid
you refuse to be intimidated
and it's some sort of friend
touching your lips now –

*

'A mate at the cricket club
in the shower after the game
felt a lump on his shin
Bone cancer
Cut off the leg
He came to spectate
propped on crutches on the boundary
Then they took the other one
From a wheelchair he
watched the last match of the season
Said we'd have won but for a terrible decision
After the funeral
we had a whip-round for the wife and kids
What can you do?'
but stare out the window of the 4.32
like the man who told me this
as we glimpsed the cricketers
  resolving
    their lunar-solar, luna sola
game

*

If the human heart
were a high and mighty bluff
set above a smashing sea
with a nearby rail link into the city
and excellent local facilities
plus opportunities for education and shopping
and a really nice cricket ground next to the cemetery

wouldn't you call its potential for development
– unlimited?
And we have seen it wasted
on yet another grotty scheme

Utterly unmortgageable at four in the morning
you lean on the windowsill
pain in the chest but still
calling the bluff

and hear at last the sea make sense
the sense you began to make
when you finally owned up and said
'I am afraid'.

This is as good a place to start as any.

So roll that log, old pro!
a new voice whispers, soft and delible.
Call him the Heretical Buddha, HB.
He speak in ital and he say
Make your contribution and then fade . . .

PROLOGUE ENDS

Scotland. January. Snow.
A mean day gloomily
shutting up shop. We see
a rusting questing 2CV
shoogle over Black Mount
wi two last-minute customers . . .

'This salted road's a black tawse
whacked down on Rannoch Moor.'
Crack! The wiper blade breaks off.
That'll learn ya, son,
                              the Buddha spat
then with a sigh leant out and cleared
the windscreen with his brolly.
Anthropocentrism makes you blind,
                     a kind
of beating your own trumpet.

He huddled deeper in his cloak and warmed
to his subject
                    (which was as well
                    for with the window open to permit
                    the passage of his brolly
                    it was bloody freezing as I
                    steered towards another slide
                    of tense and personnel
                    that lie across our way like ice)
Might as well call the punitive tawse
a strip torn off the A82, your palm
this land in miniature.

I hold out my palm and wait.
At length Bud shakes his head,
          gently places
my fingers back upon the wheel:
I read: a violent culture,
great wilderness in the heart.

    Above the whirring shoe-box
a hoodie craw veered North,
I scanned for something dead or dying,
thought of my friend Don,
HIV positive, tendons cut
by a Stanley knife when he came in
on my account when I was
jumped by Casuals in Queensferry
between the Chinese and the chippie –

    'Sure thing,' I said, 'but mine own.'

The white palm dipped beneath the blow
and we declined towards Glencoe,
hands tight and careful on the wheel.

    It's narration of a sort
when someone salts the road for us
and lets us whirr past Buchaille Etive Mor
to wind down like a clock
and stop
                outside the Clachaig Inn.

    'Let's enter. I have friends here.'

A SHORT ASIDE

Who reigns here?

You'll be noticing a tendency
to change name, sex and destiny
not to mention subject, season and location,
and if this history runs on iron rails
it's only those of sound and rhythm
while the sweaty driver whistles
samples from all eras
as he whacks new vocals
down those gleaming tracks –

Who reigns here? I say the door of the Clachaig
opens on a street in Kathmandu; say
and we are walking with the Heretical Buddha
at dusk, past Hindu shrines
where fruit bats like inverted priests
hang in dusty eucalyptus trees;
incense, spice and sweet-sour piss,
odours of sanctity churned
by passing bicycles, the wind stirs
in merely mentioned trees
and we –
              Slam that page shut! Later . . .

You take the point.
This is not the concrete world
and everything here
                bends
(when you incline your ear)
faster than plastic when you credit it.
   Got all that? Good. Knew
   you would.

Now back at the Clachaig,
two customers wait upon their Quest
for better beer and synthesis, and we
can dispense with leaden formalities
such as 'the real world'.
Let's simply say
   Inside the Clachaig Bar
    and we are.

– 'Hey, Drew! Whit ye wantin here
    besides the company of friends
    and hope of ace ice action
    tomorrow on the Ben?'

'That part of me
I left in the French Quarter.
Also: a Poet with a white guitar,
who knows perhaps the whereabouts
of a Dual Blade – our Quest.'

    'Oh, *that*.
    She went doo-lally,
    not so much a breakdown as
    a case of over-revving.
    She got committed
    and I don't mean politics.
    But at that time she'd often mutter
    how a knife had got her number –'

'Think that's a quote –'

    'It is
    no state secret. Well you know
    how lyric poets exaggerate
    especially when they find themselves
    one sip short of the loving spoonful.'

  'Yup, I mind
things got kinda tense at meal-times.
Is she
            incommunicado?'

    'Nah, she left the theatre years ago.'

'So, no visitors?'

    'Not yet. I suggest
    you pass a week in dreich Glencoe

where light is short but days are sweet.
Above 2,000 feet
        the ice is in good nick
and yer baldy-heided friend seems like
he'd front-point wi
the best. Yon saffron parka's
cool, I guess. Sherpa, is he?'

'Not exactly.
But – her?'

    'Stella? I suggest:
    write her a letter.'

My Buddha made himself at home
among the climbers of my youth,
MacBeth, Clackmannan, Shonagh, Slide,
had their table soon in roaring mood,
and as he drained the first pint of the night
this empty I
        (mere gutted vertical
        with flat cap and feet)
scribbled a letter to Stella
and some words of explanation, then we
hung out awhile, just marking place
like markers in a book, waiting

     to open

    on her reply.

SOME WORDS OF EXPLANATION

So what's I doing
in Glencoe with a Buddha
so brollied and heretical?
What's the Quest, pal?
                         Let's
                    b
                 a
                c
              k
            t
          r
        a
      c
    k
    Say you woke alone,
bereft and empty as a sheath
whose blade is gone,
and your constituent parts
(body, head and heart)
split up, scattered, gone to seed.

Naturally you are afraid.
But there's a sea inside your ear
and waves break upon that shore
and you hear
a secret sharer.
Call it heaven-sent, call it da Buddha,
call it your sole guide
through Debatable Lands.
And it says
   you are forfochen and forsaken
   you are empty
   you must find the Dual Blade
   round up the Company.

Now that's cryptic
and you might ask

where to start this Quest
and what's this Jewel Blade
when it's at home?
When you're at home the voice insists.

   Some help, but all you're going to get.
So you rise and pack a bag
with toothbrush, slippers, penknife,
condoms, passport, change of clothes
and sling it in the deux chevaux
and GO.

      Where?

Start with the heart,
last heard of climbing in Glencoe.

   So here we are, still waiting for her letter.

STELLA

The sparrow teetering on the windy sill
raps, waits
　　(I read your letter secretly)
till the woodworm crawl from the wood.
They shriek in very high voices,
stabbed by yon wee warbling bird
　　(break my heart, no love in it)
that winks then flits
in the smug way of early birds.
Lucky atoms, that know no choices . . .

Some days just to wake and breathe
is murder, and I a sweet tormented Jain
must tip toe through God's acres
hearing only screams –

Dearie me. Today it seems
I woke without my second skin.

　　*

Hours, days, weeks when the whole damn thing fits
　　leaves in the gutter
　　　　mesh completely,

Voices on the radio insist
　　every little thing she writes
　　　　is magic –

　　Messages! Who'll do the messages for me
when something's moving in the trees
　　and the stars are up against it

　　and the arrangement of milk bottles
　　on the doorstep opposite
is the wrong arrangement

and a name ripples and is gone
  like a thrown stone
    in the depths of afternoon

          *

Three birds part the dawn
  and I lie counting
    creaks of the hospital gate

noticing how absolutely
  everything is given
    in threes, these days

Numerology! (Mon pauvre Nerval
  it begins with coincidence
    that way madness wakes

      dresses in astrology
    rises to its feet
  ends: hung by its tie

in the Rue de la Vieille Lanterne)

          *

It is a healing blade.
The patient lies
on the crumpled bed of the North Atlantic.
On either side the surgeons stand.
Look East, look West –
they've nothing in their hands except
the very ordinary knives of death.
Nurse! Clear these clowns outa here,
their century is ending.
And my sweet, ailing country –

  I'm lyrical and raving. Here comes
  my morning dose of Tedium.

These Protestants mean well, I know,
but their love's not blind so much
as looking in the wrong direction.

A Journey, then? A Quest? Begin!
Come Thursday, I'll be stabilised by then.
(They've got me riding on 'mood elevators',
can you believe! Half the time
I'm singing on the penthouse ceiling,
next – croaking on the basement floor.
Think some fine tuning's still required.)

   The knife you seek
has parted from its sheath,
but that at least I'd recognise.
I lost it in some Asian yurt
when we split
back in the mid-Seventies
– that last long hectic trip!

I suggest: we try Tibet.

What the hell, it's big enough.

    *

    (It's called 'sampling')

I know a moor where bog myrtle blows
the veil aside, and on the sweet
clover of a machair beach
the slow beasts graze. Waves retreat
around the giant Buddha of the coastline
stretched sleeping on the sand,
five withered continents
cradled in his hand.

    (An ancient craft, made new)

His dreams are so loud

I curl up in
these grainy blankets
and sift into his ear . . .
Rescue me, friends,
for only I can take you there,
and I'm told
that in his other hand he holds –

You got it.

*

It is a healing blade.
State of the heart, archaic,
articulate, serrated,
blade of the future
    and the past reversible,
    drawn back across the scar
    requires no sutures
    but heals division and leaves skin
smooth as a baby's tum
and where its glittering edges meet
all divisions source and cease
and on that point
        someday we three
            will stand
                as
                    one.

*

(Also known as 'sequencing')

Come early,
            come alone,
                        fuss not.

Bring mannish clothes for me
        and thistles from Brownsbank   *The Wasted Man*

and roses from St Louis' gardens
so I may leave, when we escape,
flowers that have no messages
but – prickly – love.

These tapes I've spliced

This ain't no party
This ain't no disco
This is Western Swing

Play a sang for me, Mr Shantyman,   *Shantih, man,*

Western stars light up the sky –
Ane doolie sessoun to ane cairfull dyte –
And so sweet Jane, approximately –
These tapes I've spliced against the night.

*

Yup, it's called sampling,
patching a new voice
from all the old voices
rent in your throat.

When I was a girl I had a rag doll
but nane shall ken whaur she is gane

But this is not an elegy
and I amna tired sae much as
halfways crazy.   *The Drunk Land*
I been to the Darklands to talk in rhyme.

Whaur shall we gang
and dine the day-oh?

dum diddy dum diddy doo
Out, out, out! That's a
cry not a quote –

faithful as that rag doll
LOVE
Stella

(or otherwise, don't)

    * * *

A letter like that! She doesn't know –

Pack your sac, son,
we're leaving Glencoe.
Oh, and bring my brolly
to bend those bars.

No comment further?

Nope. She wrote
the poem is not a Sunday paper
and this is not an Elegy
and the sickness of our days
comes from an over-
dose of information
and the needless
prescription of opinion.
Shake hands all round,
wipe clean our slate and go!

Goonight sweet youth of the Clachaig,
the snow banks gasp as we flash past.

'And when the Buddha sat in his Immovable Spot
below the Trees of Enlightenment, he was approached
by the creator of the World Illusion . . .'

The Axe Man wakes, looks rough,
forjeskit, wabbit –
fuckt in baith languages.
   (Wha called him?)

Charred sodden leathers,
white-like aboot the gills,
he is something unspeakable
ben the city dump.

No just tae gallus,
bleak as Blantyre,
body back to blubber
the former Lizard King.

AXE MAN REVISITED

Ach, surely last night
was an incendiary device!
which could explain
this morning's ashy mouth.
  (To rock, or no tae rock,
  nae ither question . . .)

But last night he was
– incandescent! Was it
a gig, a rammie, a new
ice-route carved up the Ben?
He can't remember, canni
mind, doesni care to mind.
His bones ache. Wha calls him?
Wha cries him *Brock*?
  (No other question
  posed each dreich morn)

He feels akin
to the broken spring
of this knackered mattress
piercing his side.
From the depths of scuffed leather
he grasps an old penknife,
A PRESENT FROM AYR,
scrapes into rust, finds –
hard bright metal underneath!

Brock on the mattress
in the smouldering dump
under a grey and relentlessly
predestinated sky
laughs
and lights
the first of the day.
'Ach, Daith – ower blate tae dance wi me?'

  Man of Earth,
son of the Earth-shaker,

bleeding bull and rolling thunder,
mortal rock 'n' roller,
    rocking Earth's diurnal course,
rolling the stones and trees,
    speed-tormented Orpheus
wi torn leather knees –

'*FAUGGHHH!*
                              Je me lance vers la gloire, pal!'

He rolls to his feet   and Up   and Out.

'*. . . and the mighty earth thundered with a hundred,
a thousand, a hundred thousand voices, declaring
'I bear you witness!'. And the demon fled.*'

*

Bud rose:
*There are other ways than purity
and power's in the flow
between the light side and the dark.
Excise it with prayer and discipline?
You might as well fillet the fish
then ask it to swim . . .*

. . . And so I left the hospital, sliding
through bent bars, dropping
lightly to the ground, brushing
lowly by sodden trees.
Sonics, optics, motion in full flow,
in pyjamas and carpet slippers,
I follow these odd friends
through a world that may never
conspire again, nor sing
my praises.
In one's right mind,
few ways to hide.
Mist and sober love
are all that cover me . . .
And, friends, there is so much of it!

– Stell, what brought on that breakdown?
(I enquired as she shook and shivered.)

'Some took advantage of my youth
and then again
my youth took advantage of me.'

- And left bad heart and broken language?

'Logorrhoea, pal. I crucified the swine
in forty-seven Villanelles. By then
even the milk bottles were talking.'

She shook her head, accepted
the travelling rug Bud passed her
and bent beneath his brolly lit
with shaking hand the first in months,
drew deep   and blew
                              three perfect zeroes.
– Um, Stell . . .
Just how old are you?

'Twenty-five,' she said and laughed.
Then, punching her fist through the smoke-rings
added, 'centuries'
and climbed into the 2CV.

   Now narrative accelerates
jerkily as the Buddha takes the wheel
spinning lightly through his hands
and as with the stagecoach's
whirring spokes we glimpse
apparent stillness in that blur . . .
– Have faith, dear passenger!

We're bound soon
   to overtake
      another of the company . . .

CUT TO:

   Brock's pushing his luck
as you or I might push a pun
to the limit. 'Ach,
that's what it's for,'
says he, stroking the gleaming
dropped cadence of the handlebars.

A chancy man! Loosen the clench
and the fist vanishes: that's him.
He's shorn his locks wi flint,
close to the skull and dangerous.

   I knew him once
   years back when he was mega
but this world's no longer fit
for guitar heroes
any more than dinosaurs
(whom they curiously resembled
in brain power and leathery skin
as they thundered on the stage

through steam and primal grandeur)
and I grieve to see one arm awry,
one leg shorter than the other
and I guess he's trying to adapt
or find some spot to die.

He shivers, coughs.
Either way:
                    Mad Max he ain't.
But he's on the move,
his emblematic transport
British made, a burnt-out Norton.
He's pushed it till he's made his point,
now ditches it, limps on alone
with his sole instrument
the fretless bass Raw Power –

I hear him whistle as he leans into the wind,
forcing the way open like a stubborn door.
                    – His destination?
Oh, very well –
                    Nepal.
  Through the monsoon
he runs a voodoo rave
in down-town Kathmandu:
hard-core grooves.
Crag-rats & Goths hang out there
with Sherpas, cops, and double-dealers –
if you want to blend,
the colour's black and silver.
You can find him directly
on page 124.
                    – Is that not cheating?
May be you'll miss something
in the intervening voice.
                    – I hae ma doots.
Your choice.

There is a cure for loneliness
It's in the voices that keep company
your place after midnight
Here's another
Friend and cure –

> *Close*
> *Your*
> *Eyes*

Let your attention travel
guided through the body
starting at the big toes
creeping through the litle toes,
ankle, shin, tibia, fibia
and so on up to the Head Office
where the Colonel sits scheming how to
make friends unite the kingdom
and organise this world so well
and think so very positively
he'll never ever have to die –

Knock on that door
You might bring him to his senses
but don't count on it

As the Night Watchman clicks his flashlight,
follow him through the subway tunnels,
sewers, drains, arteries, veins,
lines of power and communications,
cellars, pumps and nervous systems . . .

> *Stick*
> *With the*
> *Night Watchman*

through the night hours as
he does his rounds
and this body no longer belongs
to anyone especially

any more than a city can
and the city seems to stretch for ever
the whole city beneath the city
   servicing the city
    beneath the skin

   Already the body
seems large as Scotland
sprawled on the seas without sleep
   the abdominal lowlands rising and falling
   the mountainous chest expanding and contracting
   the north and western fingers
   trailing the waters
inhaling and exhaling
from one ice age to another

Containing so many
   making such journeys
   drawing such dreams
   to no sure conclusion
while your country is snoring
and we are still reiving
the Debatable Lands
   you might well wonder
   where light is breaking
   and if you can put it
together again

   But one thing's for sure
   you ain't lonely

                Now
                Open
                Your
                Eyes

Whether you woke to find yourself
an empty sheath
or merely an insomaniac
in need of information –
now you're being *filled in*
and one or two things
are pressing where
you might suppose your heart to be

Now meet another of the company
We call him Grimpeur
or sometimes Ken
because he knows so much
or used to till he deconstructed
and now he finds it hard to say
just what it is he's saying
as he assembles in his room
and wonders why he had his breakfast
among a crowd of Cambridge swans
or maybe dons oh what's the differ
they all take off so slow

Out on the grapevine
(curling round mullioned windows)
sour grapes murmur
it's time to drink the wine
rumours of a final expedition
with his old travelling companions . . .
But meaning endlessly recedes,
'It's fin de siècle, Jack – no Quests left'

He paces in his room until
he's ready to transmit
The fax is primed with his libretto:
let's see what's coming through –

KENNY'S FAX

I am the passionate clinician, drawn
to snakes and sources, the tiniest
blue butterfly of a stranger's thought.
That is, I've not concluded yet
my Notes towards an Introduction
to an Outline of Ecology of Mind –
sorry, but singing down below. Can't come.
Philosophy, it's rough these days.
Pay's terrible and meaning dissolves,
ungraspable as tenure.
No foundations anywhere
except Guggenheim and Rockefeller.
Fame's itchy as these bites.
The dark interior when we close our eyes!
Excuse this scrawl –
                          It comes tonight.
No rendezvous but drums inside
say we'll rush to highest ground.
Now I am waiting by the watering hole
where all the passions come to die.

– Well I think we can safely
put this one on hold,
(said Stella as she put up her hair,
accentuated Goth around her eyes
in preparation for our journey East)
though I did like that 'blue butterfly'.
It's all a bit beyond our Ken.

Leave on the fax machine,
the Brudder murmured.
*We'll catch him later. He's made
his passion his career –*
                          big mistake,
not necessarily fatal.
To find the body of the Company
let's cross over to
the next page
and be

PART II AT THE UP & DOWN DISCO, KATHMANDU

Praises of Desire – a remarkably obscene sonnet? –
into the Voodoo – a damned good lassi – Great Sex
– conversations on a flying carpet – backwaters of the
Cam – it's quicker by phone – Come Together

Namaste!
The beers went down like rivers of cold
as all except the Buddha dined
on yak-burgers & dall
till we were sold on
the party-party
at the Up & Down Disco –
                        Western Swing
was played that night and every night
beneath a starry voodoo; we stumbled
hooded & jazzed through the soft dark
streets of Kathmandu.
                        Fresh off the white slopes
I had a diamond ear-stud and a doubtfilled mind
but with Bud and Stella at my side,
felt ripe to sing the praises of Desire.

    'Desire,' I hicc'd, 'gets things done,
gets the book writ, bairns born,
        tugs us up the big hill,
        and what but longing brings us back
to base when all else fails?
Ah folks! Tonight
        we tread the dancing floor
that birls through space below
        its ain wee glittering star,
and what's the rustling the radio
astronomer receives across the universe
but the swishing skirts of them
        who first came here to dance?
Shall I take issue with those powers?
    In high places, friends,

as we traversed in from Europe
by way of Baltistan
and a couple of unnameable peaks before
descending the Lamjura
                    we pushed the boat out . . .
    Now it has drifted back to hand
    laden with spices,
the lovely and the normal
redeemed again . . .'

    And though I haivered
Stell smiled to that 'soft angora night'
and in my ear murmured:

        'What language quickens our page?
    Desire & Fear – that dual blade
    striking upward to the heart.
Though there be scars
    I love them all
and tonight I'm up for –
                    EVERYTHING!'

    Yeah yeah yeah, the Buddha said,
hitched his bags a little higher, adjusted
the nifty trim of his Panama –
Desire is our condition, it is as mud
to the glorious paddyfields of Lower Nepal.
Pleasure converges on wisdom
like the sky onto the land.
        That is: apparently.

    'Then let us praise appearances
that give us excitations.
Your forebear had the truth of it
but it wasn't exactly exciting and
excitement's part of the True.
    Now let's gaun tae the birlin!'

Let these truths grow, he grinned.
But mind this, loon –
just because you like *something*
(love, truth, these carpets, the hashish
vivid faces offer us in the dark)
don't mean you have to buy *it.*
　　That may be the only bum
note within your Western Swing –
your desire to perpetuate these nymphs
of happiness: they must hatch and fly.

If you want a good time
– hello, sailor! –
let the good time have you.

As I fumbled for rupees
and Stella wrote in lipstick
a quite remarkably obscene
sonnet on the Brit Embassy grille,
the Buddha clicked his heels, saluted
the low-down moon:
　　Such is my heresy: I come
to accentuate and stress
the way things are,
　　the haill clanjammfrie,
the rhythm pulsing through the blues
inside this auld receiver.
This is another Way, to say
that this is life and life is sweet,
and hurts, and ends, and then –

Ah well,
KJ had the right of it, it seems:
'let us bash out praises, pass the tambourine'!

We paid our dues & went into the voodoo.

INSIDE THE VOODOO

Je n'ai pas demandé cette musique
HB yelled, for it was LOUD.
A Norton roared up in the rafters
where my old pal Axe Man gave it laldy –
'Hey, Axe!' –
and though his face was
seamed & hackit
            like his legendary jacket,
his sweat still blew some fuses
where he rioted as Dionysus –

    'Fuck me, it's da Poet!
    Long time no write!
    Aye kent you were a lassie.'

    White-faced Stella swarmed the ladder,
kicked in the headlight of his Norton,
    tugged his manky mane
and stared him out:
              'Amazin Grease!'
she hissed. 'Send me your hairdresser's name,
gut-bucket, so's I can send him a wreath.'

    'Ya wee blurb-merchant –
    if ya don't like the skulls,
    stay oota ma scullery!!'

    Aye, the light horse and the dark,
    how close they crop together
    the same grass. And how they falter
    when they're apart.
    Get me a drink without ceremony,
    say banana lassi laced
    wi Kukri rum. I havenae had
    yon bevvi for a thousand years.
    And loosen up, for Heaven's sake –
    tight ass-holes do not a Bodhisattva make.

At the bar I looked around,
partook of the endeavour of my kind
to get my shout in
while Brock and Stella grappled in the ceiling:

                Aye, complex jive & snogging,
sliding
   down the walls,
      the human race
most human when it's racing.

   The very cones
        gyred
               in the speakers of Desire
as the band from East Kilbride
played 'A Million Rainy Days',
distorting the distortion into something dark
yet beautiful in its analysis –

     I wonder if
        that's the trick of it,
to thrash the serpent till it sheds its skin
and comes out shining and we grin
at the sheer bloody rightness of it all.
(Some days I can do it, some days . . .)

   Like the band, I.
   How do these groovers style themselves?

'Rockin Buddha & the Forty Thieves.'

Well, pinch me, he murmured.
It's gnarly but I like it.
Oh, and that's a
           damned good lassi.

Talking of which:
a beautiful climber fresh off Nuptse
North Wall – nice one, bonnie fechter –

direct as a clean-struck inclined pick,
seized my arm to the boom-boom.
'Lovely
to see you, Drew, save one
for me, but who's your friend,
has he done something
                              in Tibet?
Face fits, can't place the accent.'

'Somebody told me that his name was Bill.'

'Oh, do the ron-ron, dude!' she cried,
took my Buddha by the hand,
yanked him from his dwam.
'Maybe we met in Cham –
                              your face
minds me of times I thought I'd die
and I was unafraid yet keen to see
what happened NEXT!
So, great unknown – will you dance?'

Ah, she was fresh & ardent as a blade,
drawn, untipped, to the quivering
point of desire.
                              Bud hesitated –
that 3 months later she'd lie broken
across the icy knee of Gangapurna,
some suspected, but he knew.
Though the joints were jumping
    hand to mouth
and the Up & Down was
    hotter than a sweat lodge
and her incense mingled with a hint of yak
    and consequently
smelt like Heaven –
    still I shivered.

Pleasure, he said, *is a great good
and if we waited till our dance was pure,*

who would get off their arse?

'O pooh!' she said. 'But can you dance?'

Jings! he said, *I'm just a chancer*
who moves on lightly as a dancer
never biding for a partner
and all my words are wasted birds
compared to this.
         Your beauty
strikes me dumb
surely as this boom-boom biffs me deaf.
Here, Drew, take my hat,
go calm your friends up in the rafters.

Now let's go shake, cutie-face.

Great sex, the Buddha said
when we met up again next morn,
a lil slowed up from the night's
high jinks at the Up & Down,
sure is a flick
from the tasselled edge
of the carpets of Paradise.
                    I see
(glancing at Axe subdued
strumming in the corner of Teshering's
glory hole, climbers' heaven in downtown Kat
where we'd been idly doing deals
in second-hand carpets and sharks' eggs
left by Japanese expeditions,
whilst nibbling glances from
that witty Sherpani's almond eyes),
I see the Body's with us once again.
Two out of three. Good egg!

'Wise guy, huh?'

    This time round
I am Bud wiser. Heh,
gather round, bairns,
for in this hand I'm holding
a traditional Truth:
            the Futility of Desire.
In the other – the heretical
            Truth of its beauty.
Holding out his fists:
So what's it gonna be today –
wisdom, or the other?

Poet sighed and tapped one fist
but we never knew which she'd chosen
for when Bud spread his palm, we were air-
borne in the cool air over Kathmandu . . .

. . . Yup, I assure you, out at sea
dolphins smile to hear
     sexual pleasure has lately been re-born
     mutual, free of fear and domination.

'Bud, you assure us of some very strange things.'

Heh heh, I like to keep you guessing
     so's you don't completely trust
your secret sharer. Still,
     unlike you former Christians,
Muslims hold sexual pleasure a fore-
taste of the Paradise you may inherit
should you invest the spirit well.
          Sex! A shining hook
               let down from above
                    just don't get
                    hung up on it.
'Christ let me doon gently
(the Axe Man moaned, clutching
the edge of our aerial tapis)
     I'm no just so happy
     when I canna touch the groon.'

     Play us a tune, my earth-bound friend,
     for we are Nine Miles High.
How fine the kingdoms of the Earth unroll
     those reds, them blues, the huge
          Saharan yellow!

                    Axe
     strummed Raw Power
and through the pain of his arthritic fingers
     plucked an anthem of those heady days,
          '*If Wishes Were Fishes,*
          Would Men Swim Free?'
     and we ourselves could not stop laughing
as we rocked the fantasy, sublime,
ridiculous as sex itself, or this
          flying carpet zooming West . . .

'O those hours upon the carpet'
(Poet murmured as she
took off her socks and looked down),
    'the hours we unroll when making love.'
She flicked a comb through her chopped hair
then levelled it at me:
        'Want to pull – or shove?'

Something stirred in my chest, turned over
like a wee beastie in its winter sleep.
I gripped her comb, raked it
slowly through my uplifted hair
felt the teeth grip
and knew that I could never
pass this way again
nor hold a woman as before
now I knew in all embraces
I'd strained only
to *become her* . . .

    'Take it easy, huh?'
  she said. 'Boy, do I remember
all the patterns from way back,
    the fingers' calligraphy tracing
      the thousand names of Desire
all over our bodies
    with particular emphasis
      descending around the eyes . . .
      Heh heh, you do look queer.'

    Remember chum,
  the lotus is only
    a tearless variation
  on the onion.
  To greit is natural.

    'We're coming
        down.
    Bud, where we headin?'

This carpet's going home. Morocco.
Back to its maker, among the Berbers
of the High Atlas. I suggest
you look there
on the next stage of your quest.
To find your Blade
you first must earn the Sheath.
Could be
when you've suffered some
I'll meet you there
in the next section.

'But but but –!'

– But first I'll
drop
you
off
in Cambridge, for you've still to find
the last of the company:
Ken, the mind.
Without some critical
intelligence you'll never grip
the jewelled blade, let alone
hang on to it.
For a while
you're on your own –
or, as the wife said before
she turned to a pillar of salt,
that's your lot, chum.

BYEEE!

The carpet tipped
over green fields
and clutching each other
w
e
f
e
l

headlong into the backwater of the Cam.

THE BACKWATER OF THE CAM

Just a bittie sodden
and squeezing out slime,
at the porter's box
we were handed a note
left by our old compadre:

Today's insoluble antinomies

Water is wet   appearing
Sky holds down birds   disappearing
Earth under our feet   the vast
Solid solid solid   vacancies of Mind
Booked up for summer
Unhorsed un 2CV –

– 'Ding doon the door, lads!'
Stella cried. 'Without us
the thinker's flipped
and only he knows where our blade is.'

We broke in, the room was bare,
the only books: *Appearance & Reality*
in the Works of T.S. Eliot by
FH Bradley
          and a BT Directory.
No clues, no forwarding address.
We'd lost our mind. Without him
we'd forgotten all the rest.

And I was incomplete in all things now
          what with the world's onrush
into oblivion, the dark
scorch mark in my heart
where she'd passed right through me
at close range –

Sure it won't kill you,
and there's always some way to get by,
but Homo Scotorum
came home late one time too often
to stuck a pizza in the microwave.

. . . Nights under the desk spotlight when
loneliness that tightrope stretches
distances no phone lines cross
and spirit yes that word is called for
though we dislike its spangly tights
sets out to put itself on the line
gripping a tremmelin pole
singing to itself I mean to anyone
waiting on the dark far side . . .

'WAKE UP!'
Poet shouted,
picking up BT's blockbuster,
'This has gotta be a Clue, for here
we have – The Wrong Directory!'

'Uh, would ye put that
intae ma ear
a wee bit less succinctly?'

'Certainly, Axe,' she replied.
'Your sonsie face wi puzzlement
is seamed and hackit
like your legendary jacket,
witness to a thousand crashes –'

'Stell, ye've a mooth
I could post a haddock in.'

'If you don't like the kitsch,
stay outa my kitchen.
A telephone directory of Dublin
when it oughta be of Cambridge,

is what my grannie cried a heavy hint –
            I bet
we'll find his name in here
and he's moved his Chair
to the Universe City there.'
And as she spoke
        the said Directory
flipped open.

'So has the Poet become
merely a good guesser, or
a Master of Reality
in her crack-up years?'

'No, but I am no longer
the Slave of Illusion'
            (the scene-setter murmured
as she ran her finger down the page)
No verbs! No qualifying phrases!
An ultimate minimalism, such as we see
in the very very short stories on tombstones.
GOT IT!'

She dialled the numero
and *there we were.*

DUBLIN: IT'S QUICKER BY PHONE

'Phone service has come long way
fae ma day', the cocky muscle man
murmured as we trudged the fair city.
'Look! A spire!'

'Is that an uplifting slogan
or a piece of architecture?'

'Push aff or I'll smite ye.'

But the duo turned the corner
and they were trinity,

for there was the Quad
and in it a tree
and beneath it,
disputing with Bishop Berkeley,
G.
   (Ken)

The shards of my psyche are come together again.

*   *   *

INTERMISSION

The night is nearly over
(however long it's been)
though the day's not yet begun

An *Intermission* comes to mind
Twitch back the curtain
– a lengthening slash
glinting like a razor
severing sky from earth

Easy to see
these nights were needful
when they're nearly over
and half the virtue of the Quest
is rounding up the Company

        *

'Understanding may well be
universal' (Ken murmurs
as he packs his books for
the next stage of our journey)
'– but hope is local
            thrawn
                specific
and keeps returning for no good reason
inappropriate
            unbidden
like a brickie bent whistling under his hod
or the seeding thistles
such as rise, swathed in poppies, by Pittenweem Road'

                (To
                Be
                Continued

as we must)

PART III TRAVAILS IN THE HIGH ATLAS

To resume the resumé – into the Drylands – tourists and
terrorists – Kenny Dalgleish – meeting the Hadji – comparing
notes on Black Houses – cheap labour and Stella's stanza
– A Carry-out Episode? – days of sweat and succour – a
munelicht flittin – a graduation surprise – one star awake

TO RESUME THE RESUMÉ

We
have all gone
into the drylands
for days, months, years –
hard to say how long
your life's been wrong.
Such time is measured by
fresh nicks around your eyes.

Times
when I for one
felt myself a jug
   (broken in three
   by a single parting blow)
forever run dry -
   like that woman who, when I asked
   why she drank so, replied
   'I live in mortal fear of dehydration'
and, later,
   'I'd have drowned myself years ago
   but for my parents,
   their feelings, ya know'

When she kissed me at the Christmas party
sitting among dead needles under the tree
her thirst was terrible
and we swayed to her place
each hoping the other had the bottle
– 'I wake up each morning,
   trying to forgive myself' –

and the streets of Edinburgh
were white and not in order
and on the windscreen a human finger
had written PEECE – GOD LUVS YOU
and it went under our defences
and she began to weep . . .

That woman with the hair
colour of bracken in late autumn,
sleeps alone and reads thrillers
much of the night   waiting
for the world
to confirm her suspicions

    'And after all, Drew, what's positive thinking
    but a sustained effort to kid yourself? And who
    can really afford to go south in winter?'

This little late-night reading
    is for her
        among others

for how could I forget
           not recognise
           or fail to love

my own and braver sister?)

INTO THE DRYLANDS

Dust on our bags and our capes.
Nose clogged, throat choked,
couldn't speak
               fair to any man:
'All bloody buggers round this place':

Once under midday sun
a golden wheel
whirred by without stopping.
Days without shade
nights without stars
even our mule
              avoided us.
Sure it was a dry
and flegsome world
and much rougher than littoral
the sand in our shoes.

They say poets sing.
There's a lotta loose talk.
I've seldom met one
could even whistle 'Three Blind Mice'.
Sing?
       Guess I came near to croaking,
there.

     *

   Dawn – cold – we stumbled through
a fault in the desert, scunnered,
dumfounert, forjeskit, boots shot,
lips split,
        our stubborn mule
the only optimist left (HB
was long gone, 'less it were he)
as we slid and clattered
down that gully . . .
But halfway in, the ravine shrugged

or the mule kinda changed its mind
the way history does once in a while:

  a slash across the hillside
  glittered like a blade
  below it everything
     bled
  green.
The mule shucked our baggage and ran.

    *

Five faces, four human, one
more or less,
nose down in that water.
Drank. Threw up. Drank more.
Lay belly-down by cool waters.

    '*Une source*,' Ken murmured,
    'sprung straight from the dust,
    doubtless a glacier-melt
    sent down to us
       by higher powers.
    This dawn is not my enemy's.'

Water in our eyes, ears, hair,
we stared at the terraces below
stacked like plates, each
with its garnish:
almond in blossom, olives, figs,
and the morning breeze
like a perfect waiter
          shimmied up
  to ask what we most wanted . . .

    Between aridity and life
    runs a slash
    the width of an irrigation channel –
    miracle, for sure
but one honed by human hands.

'Juxta
       position,'
   said Stella as she
rinsed her hair from red to fair,
knocked out her hat and spat, 'the whole
    armature of experience, the motor
    of modern art.
        If I had a hammer
I'd knock up a sestina.'

      'No, no!' we cried.
   She cracked her pursed lips,
   began to whistle.

'Sod that,' Brock said, lifted
the jewelled binoculars that hung
from the neck of the mule:
  'Woodsmoke, a village, water-mills,
    five hours hence. Ya beauty!
                –Let's roll.'

    *

Up front she sang
'These Boots Are Made For Walking'.
Behind her, Kenny ducked and hummed
'Dark Isle' and 'The Flowers of the Forest'
She turned and looked at him
and between them flew something
like a pass
      so quick I couldn't tell
who now held the ball

but something had been exchanged
and happiness was punted
way into the sky
where it hung for hours
descending only at dusk
as we entered the village.

Oh catch and wrap it in your arms
and fold it quietly in your pack
like music for a better day –
then tomorrow back to the Drylands.

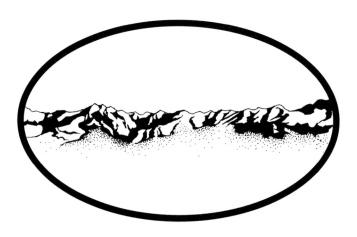

HIGH ATLAS

—~~~~ English.

Je ne suis pas Anglais, je suis
un Ecossais. Je n'ai pas fait cette guerre

Two men rose like quivers of heat
from the dried-up wadi, greeted us
in Allah's name, demanded a light.
We agree: God is good, shook on that.
But the tall man's grip
        tightened on my wrist
as he bent to light his cigarette
and the short one drew a knife
to pare his nails;
        in the glittering
I saw the three who stood behind us.

It's that simple: sun overhead,
four blades, the oddly plastic
barrel of a semi-automatic
stroked idly against the ribs.

I wondered how this was going to feel,
hoped it brief, especially for her
whose fair hair shivered in the heat
while the youngest plucked her necklace,
swung it gently in his hand . . .

'Well,' she said, 'no point
giving up smoking now. Can I
mooch one too, please?'

    '*Hal anta mai?*'
      'Whit's he sayin?'
    ' "Whose side are you on?" '
'Ooh la la,' Stell murmured. 'Such ancient questions.'
    '*Hal anta Americain?*'

'Je ne suis pas americain, nous sommes
des écossais. (Hold on tight, babe.)
Je n'ai pas fait cette guerre. (Christ,
we should've stayed at your cousin's,
the Archduke's.)'

'*You speak very bad French. So,*
you are English, I think?'

'Pas du tout!'

  '*Alors, British.*'

'Pas tellement. Scottish. Wee place up North.'

The youngest man looked up.

'*Scotland!*
    '*Scottishers?*
        Kenny Dalgleish!'

'Oui, oui. Kent his faither. Uh,
j'ai connu son père . . .'

    '*Ours too is a small country,*
    our football team also loses.
    One day we shall win, Inshallah.'

'But we are travellers, innocent travellers.'

    '*There are no innocent tourists.*
    You must know this.'

The blade lay on my cheek, scraped:

    '*You need a shave, mon cher,*
    you look like a terrorist.'

– He laughed, flipped the blade
high into the blue, where it spun
whittling the breeze to nothing,
  and when it clattered at our feet

      all men had gone

    and we were alone in the wadi,
    sweat running from our boots.

We walked on, but from then
the world was hotter, focused,
as if those men had been
                    guardians
lounging at the arc of an invisible lens.

Up ahead, distance and almond trees.
We drank a little wine and came quickly to the village,
pausing every so often to be sick.

Three weeks into the High Atlas,
rising each day
into debatable lands
where we could only guess the argument.
Hard light, harsh lands, honed faces
with manners more courteous than our own,
each with a knife
winking at the hip
and hospitality proportional to poverty
as is the way
with mountain people in this world,
as though their scabby villages
are last undrowned outposts
of an earlier, better way . . .

You won't like this thought,
but there was a war on
in a not so distant desert
and we wondered
whether chaos, like cruelty,
is a constant
that changes only its location
and so will always find a home.

I said you wouldn't like it.

We had gone *behind the war*
as though it were a curtain, a
            tapestry of violence,
and now
the heart draws it back,
            revealing

– A mule clicked down the canyon.
On it an old and humble man
relaxed, radio cradled to his ear.
'Labesse! Becher! How goes the war?'

'As always. Did you meet my son
at the souk – has he sold goats?
These damn Yankee batteries, so dear . . .'

We sheltered in the shadow of the reddish rocks.
The war went on through tiny speakers,
distorted, lost in that high stony place,
awful of course
                but not everything
for we had glimpsed the timeless village
and now shared oranges & cigarettes with him.

Dry smoke   sharp juice
all life was in   the alternation
desert war   rest in the mountains
head-splitting heat   cool under the rock
silent afternoon   sputtering radio
this orange   this cigarette
desire   the end of desire
this Berber   these Christians

  and like a knife from its sheath,
  like a foot from its boot,
  came a slight easing . . .

    'Now tourists don't come to the city,
    the shops don't buy from us
                and thus
    we can't buy feed for our dry season.
    Sheep and goats starve alike.
    Vous savez, tourists like birds
    are signs of peace and settled weather.
    O send down clouds, Allah!
    If we can't have peace or tourism,
    let us at least have rain.
    And if you have no money, friends,
    then give us a song,

We looked to Brock, he shook his head.

'Ma mind is on ma ain countrie,
where clouds like grizzlin bairns
cling to the mountain's hip.'

Poet coughed and then
with unaccustomed shyness rose.
'An old lament,' she said then sang
in her husky thin high voice:

> *Love in time brings dejection,*
> *We were drunk on projection,*
> *But now I am sober,*
> *And in my right mind.*
> *I never loved no one*
> *Till I loved that someone,*
> *I saw this world clearly*
> *When I was going blind . . .*

She stopped and stooped a moment
under the red sky, bitter-sweet,
Heartbreak adjusting her sandal.

The Hadji clapped slowly, twice.
'Though you have food, I see you're hungry.
You have water, yet you thirst.
I do not know your pilgrimage
but I invite you to follow
back to my village.'

He rose and touched his hand
first to his lips, then to his heart
and we in clumsy fashion responded.
He re-mounted and led us there,
poor, assured, a distant war
cradled to his ear.

IN THE LAST VILLAGE

'No,' we said gently, 'we do not want
to come and see you "make the folklore",
no, nor take pictures of your daughters
miming prettily in the fields.
These travesties are painful, and must cease.'

> '*Wakha*,' the old man grinned, stroked
> his lang neb. 'Agreed.
> So let's converse till the yellow rider
> slips from the saddle of the sky.
> (I am expected to speak this way,
> don't let it charm or bother you.)'

We sat down by a broken wall
around a few untended trees
in thin dry grass like clumps of hair
clung to an aged skull.
'Peaceful here, we like it.'

> 'You've noticed, but are too polite to say.
> The terraces of the old ones are crumbling.
> In empty palmeries the water channels
> return to sand.
> Now nothing here
> holds water long, the land returns
> to slow mode, half asleep, unkempt
> where once were dates and almonds,
> saffron, olives, wheat gleaned by goats.'

COMPARING NOTES ON BLACK HOUSES

'My country too has empty glens,
old walls crumbling by the sea.'

> 'We did not call it "folklore" then.
> We called it nothing but *our way*.
> Our festivals were enacted
> for no eyes but our own.
> There was no talk of "the community".'

'My folk were small tenant farmers
not much impressed
by anything but work and land.
What's left from their labours?
A way of standing,
                        photogenic air.
The land's a husk,
when the grain's elsewhere.'

    'Doubtless their sons built cities
    or went abroad. Who does not want
    words on the T-shirt
    and new blue jeans
    sold by the infidels he curses?'

'There was a cow, chickens, a bit land,
a boat dragged on the machair.
Their houses too were low and dark,
full of smoke, familiar
as fatigue and dignity. Doubtless
their eyes watered.'

    'My friend, you too have a peasant's mentality.
    I expect tourists came then from the South?'

'They did indeed. Left enchanted,
wrote books about it.'

    'Your women too are stubborn and short-legged,
    then flash a smile, making work worthwhile?'

'Don't let Stell hear you say that,
but: yes. They know their worth,
will not be messed with.'

    'Our sons retire from the grocery trade
    in France and Spain, build
    European villas beside the ancestral
    huddle of stones. I live in one
    with solar heating.
                It's very nice.
    At night the heat-pipes whisper
    my time is past.'

'Hard men, hard hands, hard minds,
softened only in their eighties
as they prepared to take their leave.
When I was young
                    we had two pear trees,
a garden like this one.
Grandfather the saddler gave me his penknife
and wrapped huge hands round mine
instructing how to graft
new shoots to old trunks. Pear blossom
drifted on our shoulders as we talked.'

        'Your hands, broad and coarse as mine,
        could work leather, or the fields.'

'I can take a hint. What needs done?'

        '*Shukran*. This wall must be re-built
        against the goats. Also some hoe-ing,
        the highest channel shored again.
        May I allot your muscular friend,
        yourself, the technician, the unmarried woman,
        each to their suited task?
        Your patient mule
        can walk in circles, drawing water.

'Pal: you're on.'

        (That pointy ball of happiness you caught
and snuck into your pack when you were searching:
long ways from home, and lost, is found again
together with a handshake and an honest trade
and eyes met for once across the barriers –
be dear now as remembered hills,
the Allt a' Mhuilinn, Rest and Be Thankful.)

* * *

CHEAP LABOUR

We spent the war in that high corrie
beyond all roads and radio,
worked long days for Hadji,
dossed down nights inside his byre,
worked hard, slept well,
content to shape another's garden.

'Sometimes salvation,
like a worthy ox,
cannot be yoked head-on'
the old man grinned.
'Anyway, you're cheap labour
while our young men are in the city
or baking bread on the plains of war.'

And Stella borrowed my penknife
to scratch upon the old man's mantle

Sweat and sleep and in-between
smoke and watch the moon awhile
flattering the scraggy palms;
may channelled water flow each day,
be clear discourse through your dreams.

A CARRY-OUT EPISODE

– So we're like beer bottles then,
(the Grimpeur sighed one night
as we dossed down in the byre),
No deposit, no return?

    None answered. Axe groaned,
    for we knew by Ken's tone
    that we were in for
        another fireside seminar
    of speculation from the thinker . . .

– Yet nights like this below the stars
(untwinkling at this altitude)
make me deal this wildcard
among the suits of possibility:
Bud may actually be right.

So, play it:

we're flittin
from incarnation to carnation
like dizzy bees
layin up honey sweet or sour –

In which case nothing is as it appears
In which case Western Man's
stoic premise and speedy ways
    are both completely fuckt
In which case the bodies we bury and mourn
    are empty shell-cases
    and the bullet's lodged elsewhere
In which case the people in the street
    have wings beating so fast we can't see 'em
In which case my cat Spike
    (let us consider my cat Spike)
    isn't a nimble machine for consuming Whiskas
In which case everything disappears but nothing ends

In which case we'd best mind what we chuck
    for it returns like a boomerang
    in this life or the next
    to get us in the neck
And Justice will be done
not by a Judge but by an impersonal
causal principle
    that can't be bribed or flattered
by even the most sleekit of cats
In which case everything is truly white
    as I saw it once on Princes Street
        all colours added by our eyes
In which case we're investigating a mystery
    a case never closed
In which case this same flower that blooms today
    tomorrow will bloom again
    when death's another name for pollination . . .

        'Yeah yeah yeah!' Axe smashed a chord
        that rattled the termites in the Hadji's shed.
        'Jings, do I hate wishful thinking!
        Sure and the turtle people believe
        the universe rests
        on the back of a . . .
        guess what? . . . turtle.
        Sod it, we're all gonna die.'

        Poet blew gently across the lip
        of a bottle of so-called Pale Ale
and the sound dispersed among the ghostly
saffron fields that lay around us.
        'So what does the turtle rest on?' she enquired.

– According to the hottest theorists,
it's *turtles all the way down.*

    We fell silent,
the last beer bottles clinked.
and stared into the night.

Deep dark secret river, on either side
ripe willows stir.
The night breeze drifts like solar winds,
bearing the invisible love-making of trees.

(Still worrying about those turtles.
I hope their shells are strong.)

Brock took up the filthy oud
our gaffer handed him one night,
found it took his crippled fingers well.
Raw Power (mind yon fretless bass?)
lay wrapped in sacks, unplucked –
'Nae use tae man nor beast,
wi'oot youth nor electricity.'

Fast by an ingle, night by night
slowly he acquired
the trance-music of the *gnawa*
that can drive out devils
or drive insane.
                    'Hey,
it's only ethnic radio,
but it cools my crazies.'

Two Tuaregs appeared at dawn
across the boundary of the village,
near-black their faces,
piercing blue their robes.
One held a gimbri, the other
banged a drum. Nothing was said,
but they stared at Brock
who glared back,
but when they strode up the mountain
he bowed his head, picked up the oud,
and with a sort of laugh
set off in pursuit . . .

He returned days later,
hirpling still, his left arm bent
worse than before,
but when he played thereafter
his fingers were quicker
precise in their pressure.
'Don't ask,' he said, 'just

dinni speir.'
            And, later,
'Yon power's no skin-deep.
Nae need to be a loony teen, nor leap
across a stage tae prove it!'

And Stella started to relax among the men,
and women walked a little taller where she passed,
and showed her how to grease her hair
and rim her pale blue eyes with kohl.
And Stella said,
                'All truth is good news
                however dark it seems'
And, later,
                'Happiness
                is not my happiness'
And she wrote less
but her hands were steady.

Ken's hands grew harder as he worked
salvaging the basic
clapped-out machinery – his mind
moved less like metal, more like water.
      'Wittgenstein was an engineer
      who loved to help things come unstuck
      and start to work, men's minds for one.'

He said
            'The world is everything
            outside the text. Man,
            it's so mean to always *mean*.'
And, after a long day sharing
the two-man saw among the pines,
            'As a working hypothesis
            it's not entirely ridiculous
            to act as if another exists.'

He became
        a favourite of the children
for they found him
not entirely ridiculous
and he could make things disappear
and re-appear,
and tie the most
complex knots that pulled
free with one tug
on the end produced from his ear.

A MUNELICHT FLITTIN
(run through the MacDiarmidtron)

It wis the dowp
o a dreich an dowie day
that left us dead choked
            all shagged oot.

Night, and the drizzle swayed awa
like someone had turned a watering
can elsewhere. The moon rose
bloody and pink, Axe
coaxed a fire behind some rocks.

Ken cut a root, whittled a whistle
to play 'The Northern Lights'
very badly
as at best of times it is,
while Stella hunched and fed the fire
with myrtle leaves, to sweeten her thoughts
when the world smelled bitter.

'Why do we linger here,'
she said, 'so far from home?
Does anyone see us
in their mind's eye at all?'
Brock shook his head, bent lower

upon his oud, scrunching
Django music from those strings.
Ken heard his faither's language rise
through years of university training
through sedimentary layers of reading,
travelling, rock 'n' roll, oh millions of words
like tiny dead animals made stone –
like the outcrops around us
that hard linguistic core persisted
strangely in the moonlight
when softer things had worn away.

   – 'A munelicht flittin, he breathed,
   and his speculation emerged
   in his faither's leid:

   Can onybody see us? I hae ma doots.
   Gin there be a God,
      yon great een canna keek through
      sae sma a crack in time as oors
   tae spy whit's gaun doon here!

   Yon Absolute is tae lang sichtit,
   and oor warld's tae nearby
      for his kennin – believe me,
   we graipple here wi dreids and fairlies
he canna even see.

He canna scale doon, and like a giant
peerin in the weans' gang-hoose,
   he's shuttit oot. He canna warm hisel inby,
     an mutterin *The bairns are raised the nicht*,
hirples aff across the galaxy.

Yon stairvit yearnin in the blaw
when ye look into the lift at nicht
   aiblins it's no you but grievin herts
   o wheechin angels wha canna slow
eneuch tae enter this airt.

We're on oor tod, or micht as well be.
Above us, shootin stars stravaig,
  the mune's a pale rider wha canna dismount.
  Whit the hell, my faither would say –
It's whit ye dae when naebody's lookin that counts.

– Ken folded his penknife.
I've been a wanderer aa my life,
and mony's the sicht I've seen
he sang, then mercifully
lobbed the whistle into the fire.

    And I
lay staring at emerging stars,
strung as I was among my Company
who tugged my brain this way and that.
Ken's speculation though irrefutable
and maistly in sound Scots
had left me low and feart. . .

    Till Axe winked and strummed
another number on his oud:

        'But aa this doesni alter
        the orbit of Jupiter,
        nor bring the sodger hame frae the Front.
        And if the sodger laid doun his arms,
        said 'Sod this for a gemme o toolies,'
        this would not alter the orbit of Mars.
        An if it did, the planets are jist
        marbles pinged roun the playgroun o nicht
        for ane saison, then back in the pouch.
        Ach, yer brain's nippit but
        ony thocht's at best is jist
        a fine example o a thocht.
        An atom's big as ony star
        and we as sma as it,
        So hit me E major, kid –
        An hit it hard.

Wan . . . twa . . . three . . . fower:
The Earth's a bride
in the gounie that her mama wore,
　　She was just 17
　　billion years old, so
　　how could I dance wi another
　　syne I saw her birlin there?

An aa the bricht stars were her dowrie . . .'

A GRADUATION AND A SURPRISE

The young men came home.
The war was over
or rather moved elsewhere,
and we were fit but surplus.

Our last task:
clearing the village well.
Brock abseiled down
and many muffled curses came back up
till finally he surfaced
covered in gunge. He silently
gave Hadji
an ancient sack that clunked,
then plodded off to wash.
The bucket went down,
came up clear.
                    'Well done,'
Hadji said quietly, 'and now
it's time to say farewell.
You have connected East to West
with honest sweat, now you must go
back to your people. But first
come to the square for a feast tonight.'

   We washed, changed to travelling clothes,
and walked under stars
we'd never see so clear again
to the meeting place among the palms.
At the centre of the silent crowd,
some holding candles, the Hadji sat
cross-legged on an oddly
familiar carpet,
and at his knees
a filthy sack and crusted sheath
that flames, reflected, seemed to eat.
The old man looked at us and grinned.

'That carpet –'
    You flew it once.
'And this sheath?'
      The one you seek. Tibetan.
      You observe this curious motif

      You find it also carved
      on Celtic crosses
      on your side of the world.
      Take it: it's yours.

Ken stepped forward,
wiped the sheath upon his sleeve,
turned it slowly in his hand,
and candlelight etched his cheeks
as he stared into that ancient pattern.

'I see,' he said at last. 'I see.
The inevitable still surprises.
Bud, I declare you've aged,
or else a master of disguises.'

    This accelerating century
    has finally caught up with me.
    Look around at your companions:
    even archetypes must age.
    You once knew me as 'The Bear'
    way back, when Poet was a man
    and we were climbers, of a sort,
    dossing round the Himalaya.

'What's a name but thistledown,'
said Ken,
'a very floating signifier?'
      'For sure,' Brock muttered,
      'a thistle by any other name
      is still a prick.'

Poet drew a shawl across her face.
There were mineshafts in her heart
sealed off for her own good
and she would never descend
those ways again.
    'Aye well,' she said at last,
    'if you don't like a duel,
    don't chase the jewellery, boys.'

    The Hadji, H.B., clapped his hands
and the farewell feast began.
We smoked and shot the breeze till dawn.
Songs from the heart, Brock played
most furious for the dancers,
great bull-shit among the ox-turds,
firelight rising, and a touch of opium
sticky on our words until
the worlds began to slide again
the carpet's edges gleamed
the first cock stirred
and we were
in for
ANOTHER CHANGE OF SCENE

Brock kept the oud but
wrapped his ancient leather jacket
round the wildest child there.
    The Imam gave Ken a chasèd leather belt
    slipped through the loop of the sheath,
    buckled tight. 'Don't lose this again.'
      Stella hummed and coughed
      as though about to make a speech
      but only held her palm out to the people,
      slowly put it to her heart
      then turned away

and we left that village
one star awake

PART IV IN MARRAKECH (Narratives of Desire)

In Marrakech – the Djemaa el Fna – a debate on Karma –
Axe man's answer – Stella and the Monkey-man – who by fire
– on the bus to the coast – Interlude in Essaouira – Fear not

IN THE DJEMAA EL FNA

> All narratives are narratives of desire
> and the souks of Marrakech
> are a pre-Modern maze.
> We stepped down from the carpet
> and I sensed again
> like scent through urgent stench,
> the possibility of happiness.
> Perhaps my blade was here . . .

I did not request this music,
said HB, lithely body-swerving
trance-drummers of the medina
who drift impervious through the preaching
herbalists and hustlers of the Djemma el Fna –
nor do I question it.
Here people like portunate days appear
to shower gifts upon you
> *but remember –*

> – 'There's nae such thing
> as a free bangle,'
> Brock grunted, shaking off the gleaming cuffs
> young ladies hung upon him.

Just so.
And all I ask from you, mes belles,
is a serious price. Thank you.
And another for M'selle.
> 'Sometimes a bangle is only a bangle,
> not more karma going down?'

No, but it's pretty
and the price is fair,
and they need the money
and a little courtesy glows
like lemons on the underside of leaves.

We went through the souks,
not knowing the language used
our eyes
and read each moment of exchange
as fair deals, fear or avarice,
written on faces in secret ink
that registers then vanishes.
We followed the pickpocket
to see him deftly even up
some local inequalities
    and in an alley pay off the police.

You see rip-offs great and small,
the rich cheat
and the poor fail,
but I would ask you to remember
the invisible adjustments
                of karma,
that internal market no one beats.

A DEBATE ON KARMA

          'I hate that karmic shite,'
          Axe muttered, testing a gimbri.
          'It's one fer the money,
          twa fer the money, three
          fer the money in this warld.
          An gin the human brew is wersh,
          don't sweeten it wi honey.
          Cash is the sultan's dawg
          aye returning to its maister.
          Some get whit they deserve,
              maist dinni. End o sad story.'

No, end of sad episode.
There's more
        lives overleaf.
I know, I've been there.

    'But *we* don't know that' – Ken objected –
    'All we see is the lemon grow,
    be plucked, squeezed, discarded.
    100 pages, 100 lives – may be,
    but little use to little me,
    when I remember none of it.'

The Buddha looked a bit . . . embarrassed.
Cracked a nut, scratched his cheek,
muttered he'd been up late last week,
in any case was out of practice
debating with mortals, claimed he
would tell us if he could (winked),
but he had promises to keep . . .
Put his hands in his pockets,
felt with his thumb,
and sighed.
    Ah, Ken,
  in that case
  all I see is bitter
  and there can be no peace,
  no justice and no remedy.
  You might as well go home,
  bolt the doors, fix a stiff
  gin, slice the lemon and
  your life alike, and stick
  the future in the microwave
  along with what remains
  of your horror-laden century.
  Stick your head in while you're at it.

We stood dismayed,
and Bud seemed old and far from home
as I put my arm around his shoulder.

'**Nivver!**' Axe cried and pointed
            to the musicians who
had gathered behind him
like ripe fruit
behind sheltering leaves.
'These guys are ready tae jam,
this is ma band

                    – I shall nivver
                    surrender!'

  Where are the fox-holes of Paradise?
    Aye, where's the fox?
Buddha clapped his hands
and danced
in the sweltering heat
to the shattered beat
where timbril, oud and drums resound
the logic behind the logos
of that great square that's not a square
yet translates as *Place of wandering spirits . . .*
At length Buddha knelt and gently placed
his very favourite bandana
round our Axe's sweating neck.
  Thank you, friend.

STELLA AND THE MONKEY-MAN

  We left Brock there
as the crowd thickened like soup in the pot
around a stir of story-tellers
that in song, mime and patter cooked up
one of the world's three oldest stories:
rich man, poor man, rich man's daughter,
pausing only for water and passing the hat.

  I recommend the Monkey-man, who plays
  the sultan's daughter, the flirt!

(Thank you, no
hashish will be necessary tonight.)
His tawdry skirt, burlesque rouge,
vermilion lips on wrinkled skin
may seem pitiable, or an easy laugh,
* – but look,*
*   look into his eyes.*
*   – A shock, isn't it.*

As the crowd circles
   like the nozzle of a bellows
and drums and pipes puff lust
   and the rich man rages
and the poor man dreams,
   the Monkey-man's a glowing coal
igniting ancillary fires
   in every man and woman there.
And as he minces, sighs, winks,
   humps the air and shamelessly
turns on the crowd,
   he seems to say
      Yes: monkey we are
      monkey we be . . .

      – 'Oh wicked eyes, oh innocent palms!'
      our Stella cried.
      'I have felt nothing in two years.
      I have mislaid the outstanding
      like a face in the crowd.'

The Monkey-man held out his tambourine.
She flicked her hair back from her eyes,
took it
            and followed
and red puffs
rose from their sandals
as they hurried through the dusk.

No, let her go. That part of you must go
down into the night with the Monkey-man.
Without feeling, the poet's world's in chaos.
He will not harm her,
                just become her for a while.

Suppose I could handle some plain prose
for a day or two.
She'll be all right?

    She comes to bits, he'll fuse her.
    That spikey, tough and oh so
    fragile woman glows
    like a filament in argon
    and each bulb yearns
    for the moth that can break it.

She never did want happiness,
that ordinary quest.
She will return?

    Dazed, singed, amnesiac perhaps.
    These night trips cost.
    Her Art wants knowledge,
  but she still wants it free.
  She won't return the same
    down the tremmelin road of flame.

Dearie me,
these muses walk the wild side.
Still my heart runs after her
like a pup-dog, yelping.
I'll keep a candle burning.

    Tonight your Axe Man rocks the kasbah,
    Grimpeur disputes with the Imam
    – let's me and you
      eat roast chestnuts
    as a new moon rises
             over the Koutoubia,
    then catch the last bus to the coast.

Being is a flame
steady in the corner of a monastery
or roaring on a stage
before ten thousand other torches

    My hair is black
    My eyes are black
    I am spirit-filtering charcoal
    I have clasped the Monkey-man

Grass is a flame
Trees burn under their bark
A dead cow by the road
combusts within
People are flames
legs arms head
the five-branched candelabra
conceived on beds of fire

    I have gone down with the Monkey-man
    and he has taught me how to see:
    the stars are flaming
    the bunsens are all burning in the lab tonight
    all across the universe lights are blazing
    Welcome home
    it's terribly wasteful
    but that's the way of it

The beggar leans
on a stick of flame
the yogi's groin
is a nest of flame
I fear nothing
These dark ways
are lit at intervals
by scurrying torches

I have donned the Monkey-man
and he has taught me how to see

. . . Your company have gone before,
further down their separate ways,
there's nothing further for you here
and it ain't polite to linger gawping.
Time to be sailing back to your ain.
But take a month off,
an Interlude before the final act.
Rent the tower in the Villa Maroc,
write up your journals and attend
to spirit lurking in the fact.
Get yourself work, approach
the skeelie skippers of this salt-glazed town.
See where they lounge like partans,
hard-skinned upon their dazzling nets.

Would ya take a look
at my story so far
while I go for coffees?

– Ya beezer,
it's thick enough to crush a crustacean.
Where you going for these coffees – Casablanca?

We always knew there'd be a place
where North Atlantic winds converge
on Africa as we went down
for sardines and cigarettes among the nets
with Abdul, Hervé, Monsieur James,
and after work there would be time
for mint tea in the Place Moulay Hassan
where women in haik sit like pillars of salt
and hooded men stroll hand in hand
by children rapt on the mosaics . . .

We knew dusk must adjust its shawl
by the Red Café, round the hammam,
and desert winds disturb those birds
hung in their cages in the hall.
'Soon all we've said and done will be
blown over the ocean without adieu.'
Salt on the tiles, crystalline residue,
sheen on windows facing the sea.

PART V BRINGING IT ALL BACK HOME
(The Debatable Lands)

The wanderer returns – a fantastic cloak – a Brocken
Spectre – Debatable Lands – Praises – Journey's end,
lovers meeting – Homburg! – The Return of the Heretical
Buddha – fast by an ingle – the Court of the Stourie Feet

THE WANDERER RETURNS

Waves accelerate towards the beach,
like grief they break when shallowest.
A black sail
is leaving Dalriada.

Your man staggers from the water,
claws into the sand.
He lies motionless till dawn
in the small rain.
It's like a flat battery
re-charging at the mains.

   That evening
on the hilltop where
his Western ancestors looked out
he slowly fits his foot
into the hollow in the rock.
'Omnes aut nemo', he murmurs,
holds his arms aloft:
King of the Scots.
   – Well, why not?
Everyone's gotta be someone
and sure as fate
in this wee country
I gotta be related.

He waits in that high crowning place
till the company rise and clasp
around him like a cloak

woven from earth and fire and air,
glittered with salt from the Western Ocean,
dyed from deep bracken and high moor,
yellow lichen from the auld fell dyke,
smoothed by waves' green sook –
ach! it is material as tweed,
coarse, close-woven, rough on skin yet
light as peat smoke from the far side of the glen,
subtle as the curlew purling
silence upon itself above the furthest cairn.

Strange cloth for sure
but we're raised to it.
As this era blows out like a storm,
we surely gonna need it.

Wrapped in that fabled cloak,
that ancient and modern
tormenting Nessus' shirt, that coat
of many tongues and colours,
whose wide lapels are Western Isles
to one side, Caithness to the other,
    whose central belt draws tight,
whose pockets hold Berwick and Dumfries,
    whose skirts spread wide about the Borders,
whose ragged cowl's Shetlandic, whose collar
    ruffs the low green fields of Orkney –

he is ready now to clasp his Company:
    singed Stella, hirpling Brock
    and brooding Ken still bearing the sheath,
each with their knowledge and their injuries
for knowledge and injury birl together
'like water going over the mill-wheel' . . .

    'I can see at last,'
    she said, 'into anyone's heart
    now I've forever lost my own.'
    She opened her cloak and showed
    below her rosy-tipped left breast
    a long black slanting scar.
    'The Monkey-man's price like Cruachan
    was steep
                but fair.
    It's what I wanted.'

    They drew close together,
my flickering shards.

'In this country, at this time,'
Ken said, 'if you haven't anger,
you've got nothing.
                    And if
all you've got is anger
you really have got nothing.

Take the rubble of my thought
and make a kirk or a mill of it,
but something honest, homely, decent.
hold me, friends.'

On that hilltop they embraced,
drew close like a masoned wall
till none could slip a dirk atween them
and their circle like an ancient brooch
was unbroken in the setting sun.

   'Jings, yon's a blinnin stew!'
Brock cried. 'The years
flee like driven snaw and I
could get emotional.
Let's hie awa
         far from this turbulent place!
The body drags and yet
ma days burn doon wi'oot regret –
oor final loyalty's is tae the pack,
no tae the cigarette.'
   And he stood on Dunadd,
body black against the setting sun
and wi the haill voice
pledged allegiance yet again
to sex & stress & rock 'n' roll –
all the goodies flesh is heir to
when to its kingdom comes
that sweet tormented reign –

and they saw not the thickening body of a brute
but an anthracite jewel of a man
flaming in an earthly setting.

*

They lay on warm slabs above the sea   and the wind
                                                    dropped with the
                                                    sun

and gazed until the corrugations of the brain
smoothed to one broad blaze
then wordless slipped into
their common sleeping bag
and finally
             they
                slept
                        as
                            One

A PARTING SONG

Across this land
trees lean to the East,
and when I woke
dew-soaked and alone
that was the way to go.

I looked back once
and it made me grue
for in that morning's mist and sun
a figure gestured
one hundred feet high,

a freak of weather,
light lancing from
the heart of the storm:

    a Brocken Spectre
waving so long

IN THE DEBATABLE LANDS

From Rest and Be Thankful
where glaciers had once ground down
like ancient grudges,
    I saw the bare hills
    and I saw the conifered hills
    and I saw the submarine base
    and all its brambly wire
and I didna ken
if I was looking at my ain belle countrie
or a disaster zone.

I stravaiged through the Lowlands
where the lights were blazing
but precious few were at home
and I wasn't one of them.

I wandered with full rucksack
and an empty sheath
tried to figure out the game
and had we lost or won.
I turned South
to the headwaters of the Tweed
and camped by Liddiesdale
in the heart of the Debatable Lands.

    Still don't know what I was
waiting for – revelation maybe –
but the many voices of my land
hissed like drizzle on the tent
as I lay listening
for the ordering within . . .

Small veins beat on the back of your hand   Rivers
                                       run down
                                          through the
                                          night

if I was half-cracked
it was in the way of a kernel
ripe to fall from its shell

stars and cobwebs hang together
                            above
                            the lily-
                            choked
                            burn

and by their light I read
lines scratched on the sheath
in *ogham,* a Pictish script that said

(untranslatable . . .)

I lay against the standing stone
peeweets like thoughts made black and white
tilted and were gone . . .

    the Kingdom is already spread upon the Earth
    only men can't read it

An amphitheatre of clouds round the moon
and naked speechless unarmed
I went through there

HEADWATERS

'Today one can only trace
the headwaters of the Tweed'

The waters are real water
however much they won't hold
still to be told
where they begin.
The earth is the real earth,
there is no other
so cold on the fingers
so close to the bone.
And these trees are real trees,
not on the map.
And the loud city of men talking crap
and the busy city of women moving on

> is the real city of women and men
> in a perpetual state of arousal
> for there is more there to desire
> than anyone can possibly possess
> so even the rich itch with suspicion
> they may be missing something
> and the poor know they are.
> And so in a way the city is
> the perfect lover,
> one who never quite delivers
> which is smack on line for those
> still young or healthy or simply
> hungry enough to love
> the addiction more than the drug.
> And the woman standing at the corner
> tan suitcase in her hand
> thinks there's a choice here
> between a bed-sit and the nearest bar
> when into her head slides a picture
> of a place where there are stones
>   never cut for tenements
> and she stands
> dumfounert in the autumn rain . . .

I wandered North along the coast,
hitched a boat across the river,
turned East for home
('the kingdom is already spread . . .')

All the while, 'gainst rain and sun
I wore Bud's quirky panama,
a black hat with a silver band,
and I took it off for no one.

Till in a quiet street in Fife
I met a woman with a suitcase
and she quite clearly wore
a black band on a silver hat

and we both stopped, mid-gest –

A GOOD REST

The Quest seemed over.
The Company had wed awa.
I more or less forgot about the Buddha –
these things happen: busy.

That woman with the complementary panama
and I went back to Anstruther
and she knew where the boundaries were –
some things fit: naturally.

I hung the sheath above the mantel
among the photos of the Himal
packed the axes in the attic
with Stell's head-scarf and Ken's theses,

Bud's hat and sky-blue braces –
all things become: yesterday and vatic.

VOICES OFF

BUD: *The final move must be*
from mythic gypsy derring-do
to the domestic
and so redeem it
        to end up as we must
living daily earthly wonders

KEN: *A knife, however dual, is just*
        a fine example of a blade . . .

STELLA: *The Healing Blade*
is no phallic power source
but a tool for use about the house,
    baring a wire
or in the kitchen, cutting bread . . .

And deep in the body
I heard Brock *laugh.*

I'd simply gone for two fish suppers
when I saw one I knew,
   strolling the Folly
    as the summer shows assembled.
I clapped him on the back.
                    'Homburg!'
(I cried him) 'Your overcoat is still too long.
Where you been syne?'
He shrugged. *Aw, teaching, ken.*

Big Brudder sat on Anster harbour wall
and spat. *Fans will be fans*, he sighed,
though I sometimes wish they wouldn't.

He wore a black bernous, which was becoming
worthy of note by the regular citizens,
but at least, as he remarked, it was *becoming.*
Seagulls wheeled about his head,
dust motes danced around his sandals,
but he seemed wearit as he checked me oot.

A fine hardening, he said at last.
Come park your arse upon this wall.
We can have talk, or the other.

Bud leaned against the Hannah Harvey light,
surveyed the crowd on Shore Street.
So little surgery, so many scars.
He cracked his knuckles, scaffed
a cigarette, struck the match on his pate.

   'Whit ails ya, Buddha?'

Nae particular scunners, kid.
He dragged on appearance, coughed up
reality, sighed.

The silly sheep keep their heads down
and end up grilled with new potatoes.
It will soon be time to die again.
Anyone who can be enlightened
is enlightened. As for your Quest –

  'Yes? My hair is grey,
  my companions have gone,
  I feel okay but
  still don't hold the Blade.
  How about some Good News?'

He licked his thumb
and held it to the breeze
and all the satellite dishes of the town
turned in his direction
and viewers saw the unsayable
until the thumb dried
and he lowered it
with a wee grin.

  'Call this wisdom?' I cried,
  'Let's go to the Happy Haddock
  if you've no better fish to fry.'

  – He flung his arms wide
like shutters opening above
    glimpsed endless ocean.

         Then all along the fatal coast
tides rose and fell like rapid breath.
Along the High Street, letters flowed
   in and out the post box, a blur
as generations were posted
   here and there across the universe
each sealed in envelopes of skin,
                    the saddest
unopened and unread.
         Shadows

struggled to their feet,
toddled, ran, collided,
       opened arms and opened legs
once, twice,
then fell back into the earth exhausted.
The howf was a saddler's was a café
was a launderette then
a Craft Shoppe and
and a thousand years of fishermen
downed oilskins and auditioned
for walk-on parts with East Neuk Heritage Ltd. . .

Matter, he sighed, *is condemned*
to eternal push-ups and goodbyes.
Everything
       is nothing mostly,
even your physicists know that.
You must learn to think bifocally,
to focus on
       what's nearest
       and the distant view.
  I advise you to ignore the middle ground,
anything within the range
of newspapers.
       Don't buy
what can be bought –
it's rubbish.
Without expectation, aid all living things.
My opinion of life remains
the least interesting thing about it.

  He took a last drag,
flicked the cig away
fizzling across the rooftops like a smart bomb
till it fell in the wasteland
known locally as 'Little Africa'
(and from that dowp
great spliffs sprang up,
plucked still at the full moon

by local quines and loons
in matching silver jackets
who stitched upon their Colours bear
in midnight blue: 'The Beggar's Benison'
and 'The Maiden's Prayer' . . .)
I'm deid done, I tell ya.
Bear me to the foothills of the Himalaya
and leave me there till I forget.

Ananda, most loyal of my companions,
the one who advised the admission of nuns,
let's hyne awa. The pines of my childhood
stir through long-gone afternoons,
I would be there.

    He walked to the pier edge,
took a last look at Anster,
and his lang neb minded me of my faither,
recently deceased. He touched
my shoulder. *Goodbye.*
    Oh aye –
I think this blade is yours.

    He handed me
the small tartan penknife
A PRESENT FROM AYR
I'd picked up at the start.

I think you'll find it sharp enough.

    Then he turned his back,
held out his arms and cried
Come, Ananda! Let us go to Kusinagara!

    One push and he was gone.
I picked up his bernous,
put the knife in my pooch
and went home.

        *

'Where you been
for those fish suppers,
darlin – Kyle of Lochalsh?'

'Big Qs at the Happy Haddock,'
I said, and grinned because a penknife,
however tartan, is still at best
just a fine instance of a blade
(and I felt the Stella part in me
living and breathing
as I lived and breathed,
always distant, always on hand,
and as sparks went down my heart
it was not so much alchemical
wedding as a *welding*).

That's why he'd handed me
what I had always had,
and the woman before me (licking her fingers)
was the finest instance of a human
that I was ever likely
to be so lucky
as to always and to ever and to never.
    And, somewhere, Stella *smiled*.

                    *

It was my 40th year and my first child
    was growing in that hungry woman
            whose left hip I swear
                repeated the curve
of the field above the house where I was born:
        I hung my boots by the ingle
thumbed the blade, sharpened a pencil,
            took out my journals,
        and looked into the flames for a while.

If you cannot bring good

It's a burning world
wherever you stand.
(Who are these figures with torches?
Where are they taking us?)
Bud knew that, we ken that
who live in debatable lands.
Look into those flames,
what do you see?

If you cannot bring good news

We are right to be afraid
who do not know the meaning of this
who do not know where we are being taken
who are swept through the dark
never seeing the faces
that hold the torches.
Where will we find courage?

then don't bring any

Born of dust
swept down the roads
even householders
have no lasting home.
We red-eyed vaigs,
waifs, tinklers, strays,
escorted by fire
we have come at last
to the *Court of the Stourie Feet*.
What will the judgement be?

waves beat
upon an empty shore

KEN'S GLOSSARY, NOTES & ACKNOWLEDGEMENTS

PART I: **THE QUEST & THE COMPANY**

guddle: to catch with the hands by groping underwater; to do things in a careless, slovenly way.

a haiver: a person who talks nonsense, usually at length.

'Scotland. January. Snow': this crossing of Rannoch to the Clachaig Inn reappears in *Electric Brae*, from which come the climbers and a prototype of Stella.

doo-lally: a bit crazy.

Communicado: an excellent Glasgow-based theatre company.

forfochen: exhausted, especially with fighting.

Gerard de Nerval: the poet who took his lobster for a walk, hung himself in the rue de la Vieille Lanterne in Paris (*see* Richard Holmes' *Footsteps*).

'. . . the surgeons stand . . .': this phrase is lifted from a fine poem by David Scott of Gourock, whose 'Now Close Your Eyes' poem is a template for 'A Cure for Loneliness'.

Sampling: a technique in music production where a snippet of a song – too short to infringe copyright – is lifted and digitally pasted onto an original backing track. Alternatively one may sample from a few notes of a voice or instrument its particular tone, transfer that sound into a digital synthesiser, and then play a new melody which employs that tone. An example here would be the 'cadence replication' of Pound's *'and the old sarcophagi, such as lie, smothered in grass by San Vitale'* (from Canto 1) used here to sign off Part II. There are several such replications here and a deal of sampling, conscious and unconscious, from poetry and more frequently from song lyrics, the literacy of a generation. The sampling techniques herein owe much to Eliot-Pound who developed the first modern sequencer. Some of their mixes are here sampled in turn. Sampling is not however a recent phenomenon – all ages have borrowed, referenced and re-worked their tradition and contemporaries for their own purposes.

Stella's Letter samples from Lou Reed's *Sweet Jane*, Robin Williamson's *The Yellow Snake*, Talking Heads, Dylan's *Mr Tambourine Man*, Chris Isaac's *Western Stars*, Henryson's *The Testament of Cresseid*, *The Twa Corbies*, *River Deep, Mountain High*, MacDiarmid's *The Drunk Man Looks at the Thistle*, Jesus and Mary Chain's *Darklands*, The Byrds, *Clockwork Orange*, and of course the sampling in Part V of *The Waste Land*.

Brownsbank: the Borders home of Hugh MacDiarmid.

St Louis: birthplace of TS Eliot

'. . . And when the Buddha sat' and **'and the mighty earth thundered . . .':** from Joseph Campbell's *Occidental Mythology*.

forjeskit, wabbit: worn out, exhausted; **gallus:** bold, wild, unmanageable; **dreich:** dreary, dark, tiresome; **blate:** bashful, modest. **'Je me lance vers la gloire':** from Talking Heads' *Psycho Killer*.

The Night Watchman comes from Dylan's *Visions of Johanna*, as do the binoculars.

reive: to plunder or pillage.

Ken's Fax contains references to Bateson's tough *Notes Towards an Ecology of Mind*.

PART II: THE UP & DOWN DISCO

The Up & Down Disco was the most sweaty, sleazy and sordid night club in Kathmandu. Its decor was red and black and windowless, its clientele as described. A favoured haunt of Himalayan climbers, it is now regrettably closed.

Namaste: a Tibetan-Nepali greeting, blessing, salutation.

'The beers went down . . .' is from a story by Ros Brackenbury.

Western Swing: a form of Country music incorporationg elements of jazz, Blues and Mexican music. Its use here is broader and looser, perhaps to indicate the Western style, mentality, mind.

'soft angora night' and **'let us bash out praises . . .'** sample from poems by Kathleen Jamie.

birlin: turning, dancing.

'your desire to perpetuate these nymphs . . .' – see Mallarmé's *L'Après-Midi d'un Faune*.

A Remarkably Obscene Sonnet: monsoon rain washed away

the only copy.

'the haill clanjamfrie': *see* MacDiarmid's *Bonnie Broukit Bairn*.

lassi: a fruit and yoghurt drink popular in Nepal.

The band from East Kilbride are The Jesus and Mary Chain, and *A Million Rainy Days* is theirs.

dwam: a daydream, a trance.

Cham: Chamonix, a centre of Alpinism.

'and consequently smelt like Heaven': from Jonathan Richman's *Roadrunner*.

greit: to cry; **sonsie:** pleasant, cheery, honest.

'A mooth you could post a haddock in': a haiver or blabbermouth.

thrawn: perverse, obstinate.

PART III: TRAVAILS IN THE HIGH ATLAS

'Dust on our bags and our capes' is lifted from Dylan's *Romance in Durango*.

flegsome: frightening; **dumfounert:** dumfounded, bewildered.

'This dawn is not my enemy's' – *see* 'Dissenting Passages' from *Surviving Passages*.

'heartbreak adjusting her sandal': 'I' is probably picturing the statue of Athene known as 'Victory adjusting her sandal'.

neb: nose; **machair:** land by the shore covered with bent-grass.

'Pear blossoms drifted . . .': in this scene 'I' is likely thinking of 'The blossoms of the apricot blow from the East to the West . . .' the close of Pound's XIII Canto.

Allt a' Mhuilinn: the burn running from the great Northern corrie of Ben Nevis.

'. . . Turtles all the way down': a way of illustrating how the universe can be at once bounded and infinite, or perhaps boundless and finite.

'Deep dark secret river . . .': this stanza comes recollected from a manuscript poem by Sean Kane of Trent University, Ontario.

'Fast by an ingle' is a wee nip from *Tam O'Shanter*.

hirpling: limping; **speir:** ask, enquire; **a munelicht flittin:** to move house hurriedly and secretly to avoid debts.

A MacDiarmidtron is an early synthesiser (cf. the mellotron that introduces *Strawberry Fields Forever*) that shifts linguistic register to a dense Scots from many parts and periods. Best decoded (and sometimes created) by a *Jamieson's Dictionary of the Scottish Language*. Prime cuts are MacD's early short lyrics and *The Drunk Man*. See also Sydney Goodsir Smith.

leid: language, tongue; **keek:** glance, peep; **fairlies:** wonders; **blaw:** blast; **lift:** the sky, air; **aiblins:** perhaps; **wheechin:** hurrying; **airt:** direction, place, art; **stravaig:** to wander, ramble; **dree my weird:** endure my fate; **a gemme o toolies:** a game of marbles.

'The Earth's a bride . . . birlin there': this densely sequences Dave Edmonds' *I Knew the Bride (When she used to Rock 'n' Roll)* with MacD's *Bonnie Broukit Bairn* and The Beatles' *I Saw Her Standing There*. The tune of 'And aa the bricht stars . . .' is Hamish Henderson's *Freedom Come All Ye*.

The 'curious motif': Eddie Irwin of Tara Trust and Samye Ling Monastery pointed this out.

'Duel . . . jewelry': not sure I entirely follow Stell's logic here.

'One star awake' is I think the ending of the Irish song *She Walked Through the Fair*.

PART IV: IN MARRAKECH (Narratives of Desire)

The Djemma el Fna is the great central square (though it isn't) in Marrakech: theatre, market, preachers' and hustlers' paradise.

'All narratives are narratives of desire' is a reworking of a line from Ron Butlin's *Then and Now*.

'One fer the money': Carl McPerkins, *c.* 1957.

wersh: bitter.

'the sultan's dawg': this mysterious fragment broke away from **'the sultan's daughter'** and reappeared on the screen for as a ghost image.

'where timbril, oud and drums resound': a reworking of Ron Butlin's *Fellow Travellers*.

'the crowd thickened . . .': this line came from Peter Drahoney in Dundee 1970. Where are you now, Pete?

gleikit: daft, stupid, foolish.

The **Villa Maroc** in Essaouira was an extraordinary guest house where this longpoem started at 3 a.m., waking with the words 'I am afraid'. Thanks to James Whaley for the Tower Room.

partans: crabs.

PART V: BRINGING IT ALL BACK HOME (The Debatable Lands)

The Debatable Lands are the historically disputed borderlands round Liddesdale.

Dalriada was the original West coast of Scotland kingdom of the Scotti who left Ireland to colonise and name Scotland, finally under the leadership of Kenneth MacAlpine crushing the Picts who then disappeared from history.

'fits his foot . . .': on top of Dunadd hill, overlooking Dalriada, is a foot-shaped hollow in the rock where reputedly the new leader of the Scotti placed his foot to establish his authority.

'like water going over the mill-wheel': Pound, Stella thinks.

Cruachan: the imposing mountain overlooking the Pass of Brander.

'In this country . . . got nothing' was said by Isobel Wylie in a pub in Leith after another painful General Election.

'Wi the haill voice' is the title of Edwin Morgan's translations of Mayakovsky. This poem owes much to his élan and innovative energy.

grue: shudder, shiver.

Rest and Be Thankful: is the high pass on the A82 between Beinn Ime and Beinn an Lochain.

Ogham is the Pictish script. It remains untranslatable.

pee-weets: lapwings.

The woman with the suitcase steps from Lou Reed's *Sweet Jane*.

'the final move's . . .' and **'no phallic power source . . .':** a comment on an early version, by Rory Watson of Stirling University.

'stones never cut for tenements' is a line from Shetland poet Robert Alan Jamieson.

drookit: drenched; **vatic:** just one of those words.

'two fish suppers . . .' this passage samples Eliot's 'Stetson' with Procul Harum's *Homburg*, in a confusion of hats.

The Folly, originally 'Rodger's Folly', is part of the shore front of Anstruther (Anster) harbour. The Hannah Harvey lighthouse is at the end of the West Pier.

scunner: sickness, dislike, problem, boredom. The surreal post-box borrows from Lennon's *Across the Universe*.

East Neuk Limited was set up to market the East Neuk of Fife. Its symbol was a life-size fibreglass 'fisher lassie'.

'**Without expectation aid . . .**': this concept of useful compassion as the only pure motivation for pursuing enlightenment is very much that of Akong Rinpoche at the Samye Ling monastery, and the HB owes something to him.

'**Little Africa**' does exist, though it takes a bit of finding.

Ananda was traditionally Gautama Buddha's body-servant, closest companion, disciple, while being slightly slow on the spiritual uptake, the last of that circle to attain enlightenment, and the one who persuaded him to permit an order of Buddhist nuns. For these reasons I like him.

Kusinagara: towards the end of his life, the Buddha returned with Ananda to the area of his birth in the hills of Northern India.

'**If you cannot bring good news . . .**': from Dylan's *The Wicked Messenger*.

The Court of the Stourie Feet was the court held by the gypsies/ tinkers/vaigs/travellers or stourie-fuit ('dusty feet') to dispense justice and settle arguments.

SWING LOW, SWEET CARRION CROW

Something feels right about sustaining and developing over many years markers to certain places and qualities, a devotion which I hope that – visually, at least! – this book embodies. Norman MacCaig's late (re)quest that I find and fish the 'Loch of the Green Corrie' for him, re-connected me to the Scottish hills, especially those of Wester Ross and Assynt which had first struck into me in childhood.

With friends and alone, I fished MacCaig's most-loved place in many weathers, over several years, and ended up catching a whole book, 'At the Loch of the Green Corrie', there. As with his poetry, that lochan is very clear and its elusive fish shine with health and mystery.

Once homage is done and we have tried to return what is owed, it is time to find one's own special places, of which 'Little Green' is one, the lochan below Cul Mor another.

We may return to where we started, though it is different now. These late poems look for actuality and connection and sustenance, in the hills of my big small country, alone or with dear companions.

Tom Ban Mor above Loch Glascarnoch is a real mountain going up, and a reflection coming towards whoever is standing there. It has always been that way, of course, and the two mountains remain one, hinged on the far shore. It seems the zen aphorism on awakening, sweetly popularised by Donovan Leitch, got it about right:

 First there is a mountain
Then there is no mountain
Then there is

Though not necessarily in that order.

AG

HILLS AND HIGH WATERS

Bringing it all back home

There are some hills and people
you will never revisit/return to
because nothing can be the same
because you never left.

The overloaded little boat across the bay
skittered on the shingle.
So blue, so bright, sun on my shoulder,
late May in my life.

THE LOCH OF THE GREEN CORRIE
for Norman MacCaig

We came to know it, a little.

It kept its best fish hidden
under glassy water, behind silver backing
of the long day's clouds.

We cast and retrieved over that mirror
till the Green Corrie reflected
three bodies of light,

filling and emptying themselves.
That place hooked us by the heart.
We were landed and released.

Now something of us reclines among those hills
and the chuckle of its water
runs among the world.

KNOYDART REVISITED

The little boat across Loch Hourn
skittered on the shingle.
We stepped ashore: late May in my life.

She went to Luinne Bheinn with our friends
and I had Ladhar Bheinn to myself,
sun on shoulders all the way.

Few details remain, but a sense
of hours of solitude and strength.
The hill was there to lift me up.

No false top. I wished there had been -
sweet with sweat and turf and ptarmigan,
that ridge could have risen all afternoon.

At the cairn I thought to her
on her own summit, loving it,
loving me by line of sight.

I set off down, exultant.
Each step flowed on to the next,
joltless, as though hill and hip were one.

We met up at Barisdale, full of our day.
Years later we parted. Dear companion,
there are some hills and people

we cannot return to,
because nothing would be the same,
because we never left them.

A DAY BELOW CUL MOR

A long climb, long day fishing
alone and unseen below Cul Mor.
A long descent till – soft grunt –
legs ease behind the wheel.

So present now, so many years ago,
that day at the urging of one friend
(*Loads of trout, you cannot fail!*)
in memory of another.
You might say little happened there.
A stag with broken antler-tips strolled by;
all day a buzzard rode the updraught;
round noon, a rattle of stones without cause.
Casts swirled in the corrie's breeze,
you knelt to unfankle empty hooks.
Just once, living flesh leapt high -
a circle widened, shone, was gone.

Close that day, compress the rod.
Coil and box the cast. It's done.
You sit a while as you sat then,
entire, unbroken, filled with sky.

FROM A MIDNIGHT BIVOUAC

(1)
D6   Dmin7   C6

Bivvying alone in the midnight hour

D6   Dmin7   Gmin7

Stir melting snow, you feel the power-

      Dmin7

filled illusions of solitude.

D6   – Dmin7   C6

In your mind you're watching late night TV,

D6   Dmin7   Gmin7

They're showing old movies of the way things used to be –

      Dmin7   – D7 –

It all seems so unlikely now.

      G   A

Is it right or is it wrong

      G   Bm   A

Refrain   When late night fears come on so strong?

      G

I'm carrying my lives in my backpack like a snail

      G   Bm   A   – A7 –

And leave behind me a silver trail.

(2) Spindrift boils, the last light fades

Across the valley snow pinnies parade

These times that you find that your route has just begun

Living for one, or living for two

In the end what can you heroes do

But resume your duel with the settling sun?

      Dmaj7   C6

In the hills or in the streets

      Dmaj7   Gmaj7

Refrain   It's the same narrow ridge you walk –

      Dmaj7   C6

A wild world at your right hand side

      Dmin   D6

And at your left, the endless drop.

To hear this and other rough-and-steady AG mountain songs, visit www.birlinn.co.uk and follow link

A SCOTS PINE

I think of my father waiting in a gale
by a Scots pine near Fortingal,
October 1915.
He felt the trunk shift, longed to be
where that wind was going, birled
clean out of Scotland.

He got flu on leave, missed the attack
that wiped away
the best part of his company.
He mentioned mud, the importance of dry socks.
He walked into Germany, then back.
After that, he got the hell out.

By Forest Lodge, wind, neglect and rain
are up-ending pines
and all that dwells on destinations.
Why yearn for exile?
I'll stand here till I know the origin,
the place that wind comes from.

QUEST

What did we carry
to eighteen hundred feet
above the road from Inchnadamph to Kylesku -
our divining rods, landing net, flasks
filled to the brim?

We must wonder how
we can bear ourselves with any honour
into high places, following our betters.

(It was a gesture to no one living,
a homage to homage itself.)

Bearing gifts in hands that shook,
carried up in one that did not,
for those days we were

a net that lands nothing,
rods bending over
the breaking light.

LITTLE GREEN

'We sometimes call her 'Little Green''
CATHEL MACLEOD, LOCHINVER

Because on the map she has no name,
I believe in the lochan 'Little Green'
and her unnumbered Assynt sisters.
By roadsides, or unvisited for years,
they reflect the arc of sun,
the pass of wind and clouds.
At night, the moon's turn.

Though it is mine if anyone's,
I do not much trust my mind.
Those ragged icons bear
the brush of this, the now
of time. Little Green?
I have seen suns in her centre,
stars fold along her shore.

TOM BAN MOR

The breeze failed, Tom Ban Mor
grew tall. Rock, turf, heather stacked
layer on layer into blue
till the mountain fell over flat,
stretched unbroken to my feet
by the shore of Loch Glascarnoch.

On reflection it appears,
look where you will, this world
presents itself in duplicate,
one rising away from us,
the other laid our way.
Before you flick aside this hour

like a burning cigarette then drive,
it seems you too live twice,
once as participant, again as witness -
see how autumn bracken doubles
and two Tom Ban Mors pivot
from rusty hinges on that far shore.

These men on ice!